Secret Anchorages of Brittany

Peter Cumberlidge

WATERLINE

Published by Waterline Books
an imprint of Airlife Publishing Ltd
101 Longden Rd, Shrewsbury, England

© Peter Cumberlidge 1993

ISBN 1 85310 342 X

A Sheerstrake production.

A CIP catalogue record of this book
is available from the British Library

Photos by *Sea and See* — Paris and
E. Guillemot, Blue Sky.
Tidal Stream Charts by kind permission of
Le Service Hydrographique et Océanographique de la Marine (SHOM) — France

Fort la Latte

Introduction

There is nothing to equal that magical feeling of peace and well-being which follows your safe arrival at a sheltered and secluded anchorage. The tensions of pilotage are over, your ship seems pleased to be at rest and you are poised, momentarily, between the sea and the land. It is good just to sit in the cockpit a while, adjusting gradually to your new surroundings and soothed, perhaps, by the sounds of the tide trickling past the hull, a slight swell collapsing on a nearby beach, or wind in the trees at the top of a cliff.

Generations of yachtsmen have savoured this timeless experience, whether at the end of a long ocean voyage, a Channel crossing, or a short passage round the coast from their home port. Eric Hiscock, for example, was cruising on the Brittany coast in 1939, only three weeks before the outbreak of war:

Then at last the sun came out, and as I took off my oilskin, lit my pipe and guided Wanderer up that lovely river in the rain-washed evening light, I tasted once again the greatest joy which small boat cruising can offer: the satisfying contentment of a rough and anxious passage successfully achieved. Quietly we wound our way between the woods and fields, and finally brought up in the little bay below the town of Tréguier. Only the deep tolling of the cathedral bell broke the silence as I put the last tier round the mainsail . . .'

Of course, marinas had not been invented then. Anchoring was a way of life and anyone coasting would always be keeping an eye on the large-scale chart for likely coves, river mouths, or other protected spots for when the tide turned, or in case the wind shifted or looked like dying. In common with most yachts of her type and size, *Wanderer* had no engine, so her anchor would have been ready to let go whenever she was close inshore.

The pace and style of cruising is rather different now and our passage destinations are much more predictable. If a modern boat finds herself headed, she can continue working to windward with astonishing efficiency. If she is late on the tide, her powerful but economical diesel may be brought into play at the turn of a key. Navigation is less stressful than it used to be, since most of us have some kind of electronic aid to make life easier when things get boisterous or if the visibility clamps in.

In fact, today's yachts are generally very well adapted to visiting out-of-the-way spots, so it is all the more surprising how often we tend to make for a recognised harbour at the end of a cruising day. We are somehow losing the habit of seeking out, assessing, and using natural anchorages, preferring to spend our precious nights aboard in gregarious complexes of pontoons which, apart from costing an arm and a leg, can sometimes be quite tricky to enter and leave.

Not that I am in any way reactionary about marinas. Which of us has never blessed their convenience when cruising, making things so much easier when it comes to shopping, topping up with fuel and water, or simply having a shower and a meal ashore. Berthing alongside also has advantages if you are cruising with children aboard, although most youngsters enjoy the routine of ferrying with the dinghy, and this can teach them the basics of boat-handling at an early age. No, I am not anti-marina as such; it's just that many crews seem to miss some of the fundamental pleasures of coasting, by restricting themselves to the well-trodden routes between organised ports-of-call.

My intention with this book has been to cover as many of the *natural anchorages* as possible around the whole of the Brittany coast, starting near Cherbourg, which is just outside Brittany, and then working west and south right round the Brest peninsula, into the Bay of Biscay, and down as far as the Loire estuary. *'Secret Anchorages of Brittany'* is based on a long running series of articles which I originally compiled for *Practical Boat Owner* magazine. After the series had run its course, I received a large number of requests to collect all the anchorages together in one volume, and this I have now been able to do. Clearly I have not picked up every feasible hideaway on this intricate coast, so any useful additions or corrections will always be gratefully received, if you could spare the time to drop a short note to *PBO*, or to the publishers *Waterline Books*.

I should point out that this is not a pilot in the normal sense, in that it covers only those natural havens where you can lie to your own anchor. For the north coast of Brittany at least, *'Secret Anchorages of*

Brittany' is complementary to my pilot and cruising guide *'North Brittany and Channel Islands Cruising',* which is published by *Yachting Monthly.* 'Secret Anchorages' picks up with those spots that the pilot book, for simple reasons of space, cannot reach; it also extends well down the Biscay coast, thereby covering, North, West and South Brittany in the one volume.

Some of the anchorages will only be safe under certain conditions of wind and weather; some will be tenable at neaps but not at springs; some are restricted to shoal-draught boats, or to keel boats that can rig drying-legs. While I have tried to give guidance on these factors, I have also aimed for brevity in the directions, in order to include as many anchorages as possible. I have assumed throughout that the reader will be cruising with a good selection of large-scale Admiralty Charts, and I have listed those charts which I consider most useful for each section of coast covered by the book. In some cases the French equivalent of our Admiralty Charts, published by the redoubtable *Service Hydrographique et Océanographique de la Marine* (SHOM), are preferable for their large-scale coverage of a particular area, and I have recommended these (SHOM) charts where appropriate.

When anchoring off the North Brittany coast in particular, the considerable range of tide needs to be taken into account, both for the obvious reasons of allowing sufficient scope of cable, but also because the shelter an anchorage affords from swell may be markedly different at different states of the tide. In many North Brittany anchorages, you'll get the best shelter near low water, especially at springs. Then, you can often find yourself almost land-locked by a cordon of natural breakwaters — drying rocks which have been exposed on the ebb to provide increasing protection from swell. By the same token, if you arrive at an anchorage near low water and all seems snug, be prepared for an increase in motion as the flood comes back, especially for the two hours either side of high water.

One important question about natural anchorages is whether they are feasible to leave at night if a wind shift should force you to clear out. In some cases I have indicated where an anchorage is completely safe to leave at night or, conversely, where it is dangerous to do so.

When anchoring in rivers or shallow bays anywhere on the Brittany coast, it's important to steer well clear of oyster or mussel beds, of which there are many. Shellfish cultivation represents a significant part of the Brittany economy, and a hefty great CQR or a couple of iron bilge keels settling on an area of young oysters will not endear you to the local population.

Oyster and mussel beds are usually shown on large scale charts and will probably be marked in any case by forests of withies. There are important areas of shellfish beds off Cancale; in the Baie de la Fesnaie just east of Cape Fréhel; in the Anse de Paimpol and parts of the Trieux estuary; in the Tréguier River; in the Morlaix and Penzé estuaries; at L'Abervrac'h not far above the marina, and in the upper reaches of the river above Pointe Cameuleut; in the upper reaches of L'Aberbenoit. Take great care when deciding where to fetch up, and don't forget that those tempting menus of *fruit de mer* have all got to be supplied from somewhere.

Anchoring in some sheltered cove for the night can bring the obvious benefits of greater seclusion, peace and quiet, and freedom from men with clipboards asking for harbour dues. Yet it also offers something more intangible, a return to that sense of being in touch with the sea and the weather which is somehow lost when you secure to a pontoon, plug in the shore-power and step ashore to another marina complex with facilities laid on. Swinging to your own anchor and cable, you can somehow gauge more easily those subtle shifts in wind strength and direction which may bear upon the strategy of tomorrow's passage.

Acknowledgements

My thanks to George Taylor, Editor of *Practical Boat Owner,* and to John Kitching, the magazine's Production Editor, for all their work on the original series of articles. Thanks also to those cruising yachtsmen who have kindly written to me with comments, corrections and additions.

Contents

Chapter 1
Cap de la Hague to Anse de Paimpol
excluding the Channel Islands

The pronounced bight in the north coast of France between Cap de la Hague and the Anse de Paimpol is often known as the Gulf of St Malo. This is the fascinating and popular cruising ground which contains the Channel Islands and Iles Chausey, although I don't cover any of the Channel Island anchorages in this book — they would run to quite a sizeable volume of their own. Also, I think it's true to say that the anchorages of the mainland coast are generally less well known than those of the Channel Islands, since visiting yachts in this area are usually cruising with limited time and tend to hop between the main ports-of-call which are most prominent in pilot books.

Although the Gulf of St Malo is renowned for its powerful tides and copious rocks, you soon get used to passage planning with this in mind. Fast tides, in themselves, cause no great problems; they can, indeed, be turned to considerable advantage, making for surprisingly fast passage times if you judge your departures and arrivals carefully. Decca and GPS now alleviate the stress of navigational uncertainty for many yachtsmen, so that the main danger caused by fast tides is their effect on sea state locally. Certain parts of the area are notorious for overfalls, especially with a weather-going stream and at springs. This is particularly true of the northern gateway to these waters, the Alderney Race.

Even a moderate wind over the tide creates nasty overfalls in the Alderney Race, so it's wise to go through as near slack water as possible. Ideally, yachts bound south should arrive at a position about two miles north-west of Cap de la Hague half an hour before HW Dover i.e. about 4½ hours *after* HW St Helier. It is then slack water in the Race, but the south-west stream will be just about to start in your favour. Yachts coming north to leave the area face a trickier problem of timing, since it's important to carry the fair north-going tide but to clear Cap de la Hague by an hour before HW Dover i.e. four hours after HW St Helier.

Passages under sail within and across the Gulf of St Malo can usually be worked in six-hour stretches i.e. taking a full tide per leg. So that, for example, you can reckon about a tide each from Cherbourg to Guernsey, from Guernsey to Jersey, from Jersey to Granville or St Malo and so on. In this respect, fast motor boats have a certain amount of flexibility about passage timing, although it's generally even more important that they avoid heavy overfalls and hence time their arrival in potentially turbulent areas for as near slack water as possible.

While the Alderney Race is the most infamous tidal sluice in the Gulf of St Malo, there are several other 'gates' through which you need to time your passage carefully. The Swinge, between Alderney and Burhou, should always be treated with respect; a wind over tide here — especially a south-westerly or westerly against a south-west going stream — can give a yacht a rough ride from which there's no turning back. Sailing south-west from Alderney, it's best to leave Braye harbour about 2½ hours after HW St Helier to catch slack water in the Swinge. Yachts approaching the Swinge from the direction of Guernsey will probably have carried the north-going stream up from the Little Russel and should aim to arrive opposite Burhou by 2½ hours after HW St Helier.

The Little Russel is the relatively narrow channel between Guernsey and Herm. The streams are strong in the Little Russel, especially at its north end, reaching six knots at springs near Roustel beacon-tower. With the uneven sea bed, a weather-going tide kicks up some nasty overfalls locally. Some of the most malevolent conditions can be experienced on the north-going stream in a two-reef north-easterly. Many homeward bound crews have hankered after the tranquillity of St Peter Port, left with bravado half-an-hour before, as they are swept through steep breaking seas at the north end of the Little Russel.

Down on the Brittany mainland, there are powerful streams around the south-west corner of the Gulf of St Malo, especially near Plateau des Roches Douvres and in the outer approaches to the Lézardrieux River between Les Heaux lighthouse and the dangers seaward of Ile de Bréhat. In the Baie de St Brieuc the streams are more moderate but then, further east, you get a strong sweep across the outer approaches to St Malo itself. In the south-east corner of the gulf, the Baie de Mont St Michel is a notorious area of strong tides, especially on a spring flood. Yachts are advised to stay well out of this potentially treacherous bay, except for the anchorages on the north-west side near Cancale.

The east side of the Gulf of St Malo, between Cap de la Hague and Mont St Michel, is actually in Normandy, not Brittany. This can be a rather tricky and inhospitable coast, with much of it quite shallow for several miles offshore. The inshore streams are more moderate than elsewhere in the Gulf, until you get up near Cap de la Hague and the Alderney Race. Granville is the most accessible yacht harbour, right down in the south; further north, shoal draught boats can get into Diélette, Carteret and Portbail. I have included a couple of fine weather anchorages near Cap de la Hague — one to the south and one to the east — which can be useful while waiting for a fair tide, or simply to escape from the throng in high season. Anse Pivette, just east of Nez de Jobourg, lies right on the boundary of a prohibited anchorage area opposite the nearby Atomic Energy Centre. Although this exclusion seems forbidding, I have had no problems anchoring in this delightful bay, from which a path winds up the cliffs to a small restaurant.

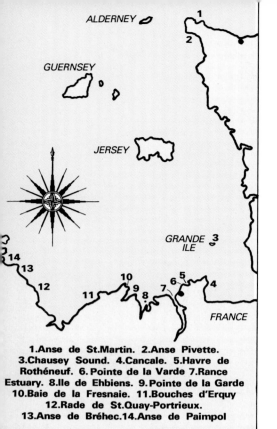

1. Anse de St. Martin. 2. Anse Pivette.
3. Chausey Sound. 4. Cancale. 5. Havre de
Rothéneuf. 6. Pointe de la Varde 7. Rance
Estuary. 8. Ile de Ehbiens. 9. Pointe de la Garde
10. Baie de la Fresnaie. 11. Bouches d'Erquy
12. Rade de St. Quay-Portrieux.
13. Anse de Bréhec. 14. Anse de Paimpol

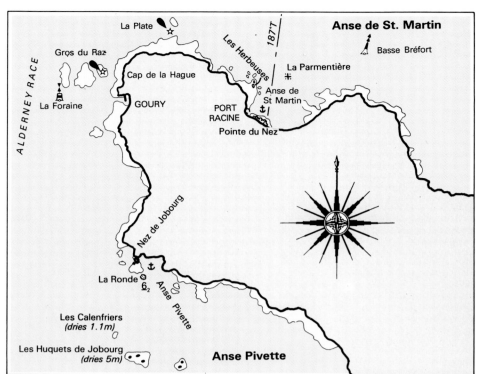

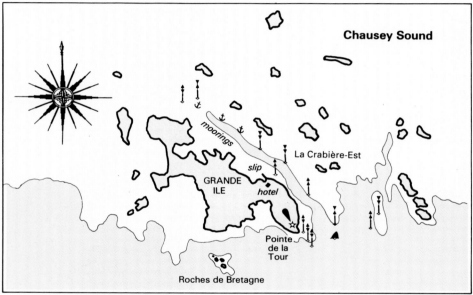

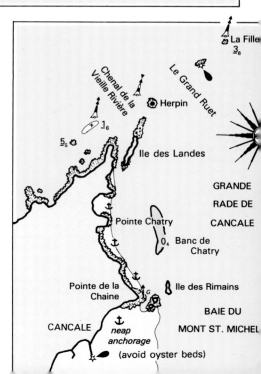

PART 1 — CHERBOURG TO PAIMPOL, excluding the Channel Islands

Anse de St Martin: A couple of miles E of Cap de la Hague, this bay offers a possible anchorage for anyone awaiting a fair tide through the Alderney Race or, in settled weather, for an overnight stop. Reasonable holding in sand and sheltered from W through S to SE.

In westerlies, fetch up about 1½ cables E of Port Racine breakwater. On the approach, pick out Pointe du Nez — a low promontory at the W end of the sandy beach at the head of the bay — and keep it bearing 187°T to leave La Parmentière (awash at LAT) 1½ cables to the E and Les Herbeuses (above-water rocks 3-10m high) about 2 cables to the W.

Anse Pivette: Lying close E of Nez de Jobourg, this tiny bay offers good shelter in winds between N and E, clear of the powerful streams of the Alderney Race. Approach from a position ¾ mile SW of Nez de Jobourg, preferably at slack water, leaving Les Calenfriers (dries 1.1m) and Les Huquets de Jobourg (dries 5m) well to the S.

Enter the bay from E of S having skirted La Ronde, a tail of drying rocks extending nearly ¼ mile S of the Nez. Tuck in close, fetching up in about 3-4m.

Chausey Sound: This narrow channel lies between Grande Ile Chausey and the mass of drying reefs to the N and E. Good shelter from all winds at LW, but uncomfortable near HW in fresh weather from NW or SE. Streams are fast in the Sound at half-tide, so care is needed when planning trips ashore in the dinghy. The NW part of the Sound dries at LAT and there is greater scope for anchoring at neaps. There are some visitors' moor-

ings in the reach opposite the NE corner of Grande Ile, crowded at weekends.

Entry is straightforward from the S, between three E-cardinal beacons off Pointe de la Tour and a green conical buoy on the E side of the fairway. The N entrance requires careful pilotage and is navigable from 2½ hrs before to 1½ hrs after HW.

Cancale: Although Cancale harbour dries at half-ebb, there are several possible anchorages off the coast to the N, depending on wind direction and the height of tide. At dead neaps and in quiet or westerly weather, boats of moderate draught can stay afloat 2-3 cables SSW of Pointe de la Chaine. You can land at the beach and the town is nearby.

There are three shallow bays between Pointe de la Chaine and Pointe du Grouin, any of which can be used by keel boats in winds from NW through W to S. Good holding in sand and mud, but tuck in close to

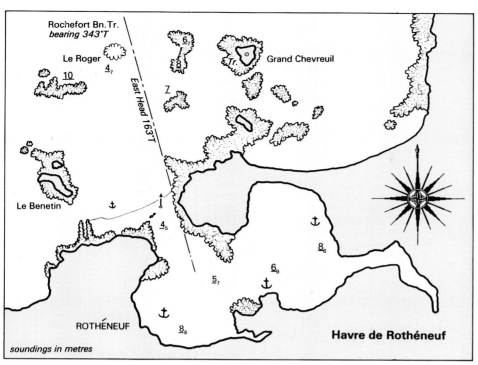

avoid the worst of the tidal stream. The approach is straightforward, either from the N via le Grand Ruet or the Chenal de la Vieille Rivière, or directly into the Grande Rade de Cancale from the NE.

Havre de Rothéneuf: The narrow entrance to this large natural inlet lies midway between Pointe du Meinga and Pointe de la Varde. Rothéneuf dries, but there are various sandy beaches where suitable boats can take the ground in perfect shelter. One of the best spots is in the SW corner of the inlet, close inshore with Rothéneuf church spire bearing about WSW.

Approach near HW from a position ½ mile S of Rochefort W-cardinal beacon tower and bring the edge of the E head of the entrance to bear 163°T (Rochefort bearing 343°T astern). Follow this line and pass close E of a post beacon which stands in the middle of the entrance. Patches of drying rocks lie either side of the approach, so allow carefully for any cross-tide.

Pointe de la Varde: There is a tiny, daytime anchorage just E of Pointe de la Varde,

St Servan (Ause de Solidor)

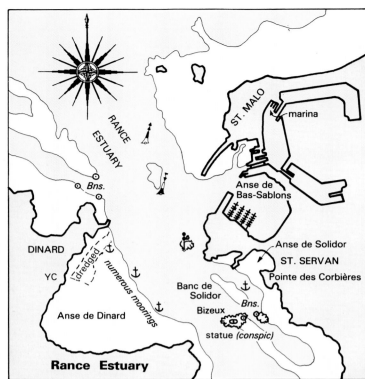

Rance Estuary

sheltered in winds with any S in them. Follow the charted marks for the Chenal de la Bigne and turn off at La Varde. An overnight stop is not recommended, because it is almost impossible to find a safe way out in the dark if you have to.

Rance Estuary: There are two possible anchorages between St Malo and the Rance barrage; off St Servan in Solidor Bay, on the E side of the estuary, or off the Anse de Dinard on the W side. The best spot in Solidor Bay is about a cable due W of Pointe des Corbières, inside Solidor Bank. The Anse de Dinard dries right out at springs, but you can tuck well into the N corner at neaps.

River Rance: There are numerous attractive anchorages in the river above the barrage. Tuck close inshore to avoid the current

and bear in mind that the rise and fall is rapid when the tidal generators are operating. In the upper reaches, between St Suliac and Mordreux, keel boats need to pick their spot with care, sounding carefully before anchoring. There is a useful deep-water pool just below the suspension bridge at Port St Hubert.

Ile des Ehbiens: There is a delightful sheltered anchorage off the S side of this small private island, which lies 2½ miles ESE of Pointe de St Cast and can be identified by its prominent tower (33m high). Approach from due N at any state of tide, leaving Porte des Ehbiens (an above-water rock 8m high) a good cable to the W and Platus isolated danger beacon a cable to the E.

Sound carefully on the way in, fetching up a little way into the bay (dries at LAT) formed

by the S shore of the island and the narrow promontory which extends towards Pointe du Chevet. There are numerous rocky dangers between the tip of this spur and Pointe du Chevet. Near springs, anchor off the SE corner of the island in 1m LAT.

Pointe de la Garde: In moderate westerly weather, there is an anchorage close SE of Pointe de la Garde, 1¾ miles W of Ile des Ehbiens. A clear approach from the NE, with fair holding in sand (1.2m LAT). There is a landing slip on the SE side of the point.

Baie de la Fresnaie: The entrance lies 2 miles SE of Cap Fréhel. Most of the bay dries and is taken up with mussel beds, but there is a shallow anchorage on the W side of its mouth, a couple of cables SSW of Pointe de la Cierge. On several occasions I have edged my

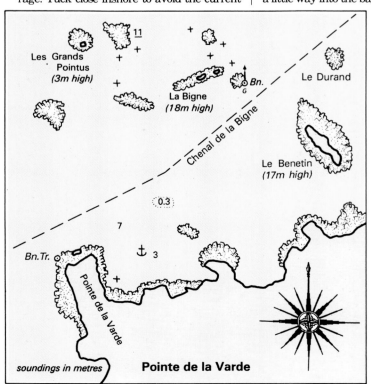

soundings in metres

Pointe de la Varde

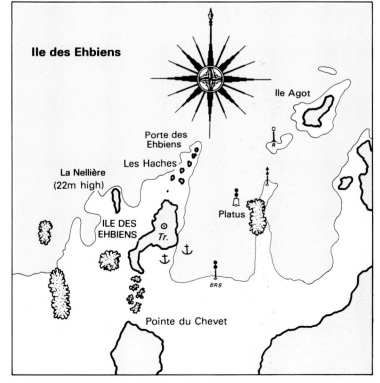

Ile des Ehbiens

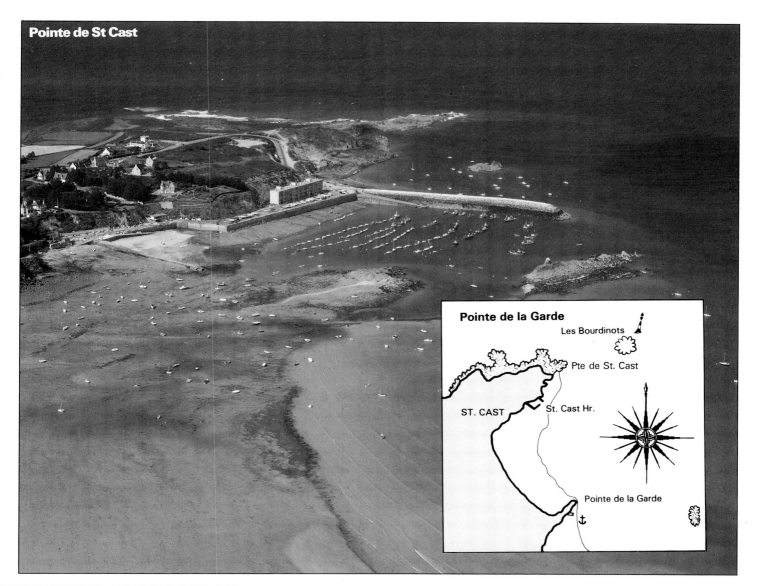

Pointe de St Cast

Pointe de la Garde

Les Bourdinots

Pte de St. Cast

ST. CAST

St. Cast Hr.

Pointe de la Garde

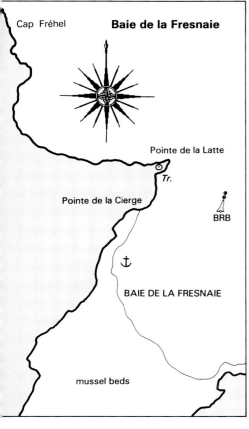

Cap Fréhel

Baie de la Fresnaie

Pointe de la Latte

Tr.

Pointe de la Cierge

BRB

BAIE DE LA FRESNAIE

mussel beds

way in here in murky visibility, first closing from the E with Pointe de la Latte and its easily identified fort, and then sounding into the bay close along the W shore. Sheltered in winds from NW through W to S, with good holding in sand and mud.

There is also an anchorage just S of Pointe de la Latte itself, used sometimes by French yachts and sheltered broadly from the W. I find this rather a forbidding spot though, and there are often overfalls and tidal eddies off the headland.

Bouches d'Erquy: This off-beat anchorage makes an interesting diversion if you are on your way W to Erquy, or perhaps to Binic, although it should only be approached in quiet weather or when the wind is in the S. From Cap Fréhel, come onto line for the Chenal d'Erquy, but turn shorewards just before Plurien church spire bears 180°T. Head towards the long, sandy beach fronting Sables d'Or-les-Pins, keeping Plurien spire bearing a little over 180°T. Leave Ile St Michel (with its small chapel) ¾ mile to starboard and Rocher Bénard (a conical above-water rock close inshore) 2-3 cables to port. When Ile St Michel is abaft the beam, head SW for the W end of the dunes and fetch up in about 2m. An alternative anchorage is off Port Barrier, 2 cables SSW of Rocher Bénard.

Rade de St Quay-Portrieux: This really comes under the 'harbour' category, but is worth bearing in mind as a reasonably secure anchorage on the W side of the Baie de St Brieuc. The Rade lies SSE of the new marina, between Portrieux old harbour (which dries) and the string of drying rocks and islets, a mile offshore, known as Roches de St Quay. These make the area unsafe in poor vis.

The moderate streams flow NW-SE through the Rade, only touching 2 knots during the middle hours of a spring flood. Anchor 4-5 cables ESE of Portrieux pierheads, with Le Four white beacon tower bearing SW about 2-3 cables. Good shelter from NW through W to S, and Roches de St Quay offer limited protection in moderate winds between NE and E. The approach from northward is straightforward in good visibility, using Ile Harbour and Madeux W-cardinal beacon tower as the key marks and referring to Admiralty Chart No 3672.

Anse de Bréhec: This pleasant sandy bay lies just over 3 miles S along the coast from Lost-Pic lighthouse and the Anse de Paimpol. Le Taureau beacon tower is a useful mark, standing on an isolated rock ¾ mile due E of Bréhec. There is also a prominent white tower on the cliffs 1½ miles SE of the entrance.

The bay has numerous local moorings and

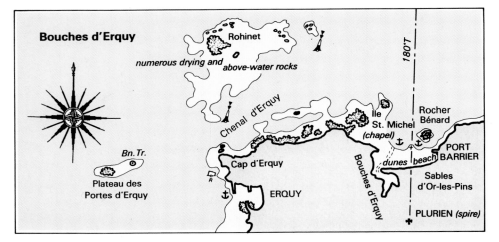

Bouches d'Erquy

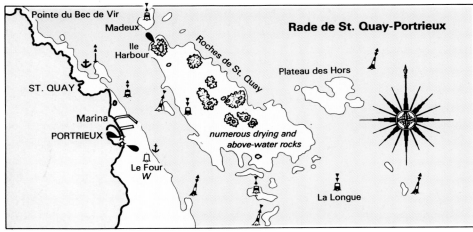

Rade de St. Quay-Portrieux

Paimpol

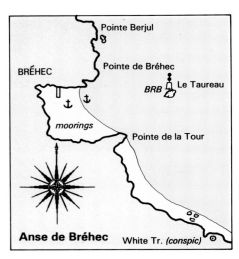

Anse de Bréhec

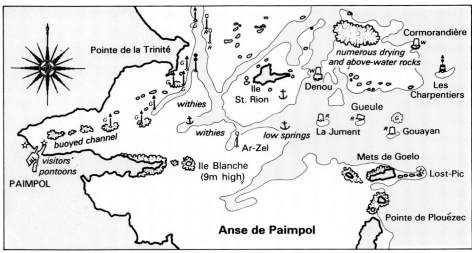

Anse de Paimpol

the small resort of Bréhec lies at its head. Good shelter in winds from NNW through W to S. Tuck as close inshore as possible, but most keel boats will need to anchor ¼ mile E of Bréhec jetty to stay afloat at MLWS.

Anse de Paimpol: This wide shallow bay is one of the most attractive on the North Brittany coast. Facing E, it is straightforward to approach from that direction in reasonable visibility, between Lost-Pic lighthouse and Les Charpentiers E-cardinal beacon tower. The streams run strongly NNW-SSE off the entrance, but are generally weak once you are inside Lost-Pic, except near Pointe de la Trinité. Most of the bay westward of Ile St Rion dries or is very shallow at LAT, so neap tides provide the best choice of anchorages.

You can anchor about 3 cables SSE of Ile St Rion between neaps and springs, but make sure you are E of the withies marking the oyster beds. Good shelter from N through W to S.

Further inshore, there is a neap anchorage due S of Pointe de la Trinité, not quite ½ mile N of Ile Blanche. Using Admiralty Chart No 3673, you need to locate the narrow channel which leads towards the head of the bay, picking your way between the oyster beds with their dense patches of withies.

If you arrive in the Anse de Paimpol near LWS, you can fetch up 3-4 cables W of La Jument red beacon tower. Coming into the bay, skirt N of Gouayan red beacon tower, Rocher Gueule red can buoy and La Jument, and then keep Rocher Gueule red can buoy just open to the N of La Jument. Continue slowly shorewards on this transit, anchoring when you run out of water. You can start to approach Paimpol harbour about 2 hours before local HW. ●

Useful Admiralty Charts
No 1106 — Approaches to Cherbourg
No 3653—Guernsey to Alderney and the adjacent coast of France
No 3656 — Plateau des Minquiers and the adjacent coast of France
No 3659 — Cap Fréhel to Iles Chausey
No 3672 — Harbours on the NW coast of France
No 3673 — Lézardrieux and Paimpol with approaches
No 3674 — Lost-Pic to Cap Fréhel

Chapter 2
Anse de Paimpol to La Penzé River

The 50 miles of coastline between the Anse de Paimpol and La Penzé River takes in the whole of the dramatic Côte de Granit Rose and a bit more besides. This is archetypal North Brittany, starting at the eastern end with the timeless estuaries of the Lézardrieux and Tréguier rivers, both littered with rocky dangers at their mouths but mellowing quickly as they wind inland between wooded banks to penetrate well into rural France. Westwards from the Tréguier estuary, a string of small harbours hemmed in by rocks — Port Blanc, Perros-Guirec, Ploumanac'h, Trégastel, Trébeurden — offers some intriguing anchorages until you reach the shallow Lannion River, with its sheltered pool off Le Yaudet. This really marks the end of the Côte de Granit Rose; further west, between Lannion and the wide Morlaix estuary, the cliffs are a more familiar granite grey.

Although some of the most popular North Brittany harbours lie along this stretch of coast, there is still plenty of scope, even in high season, for finding quiet anchorages away from the crowds. The rivers usually offer the most reliable protection for an overnight stop in uncertain weather, but there are also several natural hideaways in sheltered bays and behind headlands where you can drop the hook safely given a half reasonable forecast.

Passage-making along this coast is fairly straightforward, so long as you aim to carry sufficient fair tide. You'll come across the most powerful streams — up to five or six knots at springs — in the approaches to the Lézardrieux estuary between Les Heaux and La Horaine lighthouses, as the tide pours round this corner of North Brittany to fill and empty the Gulf of St Malo. The stream also tends to accelerate in the relatively narrow strait between Les Sept Iles and the mainland near Ploumanac'h, getting up to four knots at springs south of Ile aux Moines during the middle hours of the tide.

Working west under sail from Lézardrieux, it's difficult for most boats to carry a full tide right along to the Morlaix estuary, partly because of the longish haul out of the Lézardrieux estuary and round Les Heaux to start with. Better to make two shorter hops — from Lézardrieux to Perros, Ploumanac'h or Les Sept Iles say, and thence to Morlaix on the next tide.

Swell can be a more significant factor along this coast than in the Gulf of St Malo, as you edge nearer the outer approaches of the English Channel. An Atlantic swell from due west doesn't usually carry this far up-Channel close inshore, but a partly onshore swell caused by prolonged north-westerlies can find its way into many of the otherwise quite protected anchorages covered in this chapter.

The atmosphere and character of the natural anchorages between the Anse de Paimpol and the Penzé River vary a good deal. On the one hand are the peaceful upper reaches of the rivers, where you can fetch up far enough inland to enjoy perfect shelter whatever is happening at sea, but still stay afloat at any state of tide. Lézardrieux and Tréguier offer the best choice in this respect, and there is nothing quite so soothing, to my mind, than lying at anchor for a few days surrounded by wooded hills, farmland and the placid routines of the country. The subtle sounds and smells of a river often make a welcome contrast to the harsh flavours of the sea, yet you know that, at short notice, you can slip downstream to open water and the prospect of new destinations.

On the other hand, you have the more tenuous coastal anchorages which are perfectly snug in the right conditions but may change mood rather quickly if the wind should shift or freshen. Les Sept Iles, the Trébeurden anchorages and Locquirec fall into this category, with Sept Iles the easiest to leave after dark if necessary. A night at anchor in the bay between Ile aux Moines and Ile Bono can be an eerie experience. Right next door, the three powerful beams of Ile aux Moines lighthouse sweep the black horizon every 15 seconds. There are no other lights on Sept Iles, and the distant homely glimmer from windows on the mainland at Perros-Guirec somehow enhances the solitude of the anchorage.

Twenty miles south-west of Les Sept Iles, the Morlaix and Penzé estuaries offer one or two secluded anchorages which are only rarely sampled by yachts on passage. Pen Lann is the recognised holding anchorage at the mouth of the Morlaix River, a safe spot to wait for the tide before heading upstream to catch the lock into Morlaix basin. You can usually lie comfortably at Pen Lann overnight, reasonably protected from seaward by the headland, Ile Louet just to the north, and by the cordon of reefs out in the estuary. In calm weather or offshore winds, however, there is also scope for anchoring on the north side of Pen Lann, more or less opposite Carantec. Despite the scale of its estuary, the Morlaix river itself dries to mud only a couple of miles above Pen Lann and is therefore rather limited for anchoring.

The shallow Anse de Térénez, over on the east side of the Morlaix estuary, makes an interesting anchorage near neaps. It is better protected than Pen Lann with the wind anywhere in the south and the small hamlet ashore has a friendly atmosphere. Just to the west of the Morlaix estuary, the Penzé is probably one of the least visited rivers in North Brittany. You need to go up above half-tide, follow the channel carefully and avoid the various patches of oyster bed withies on the way. The reward for this slightly delicate pilotage is peace and quiet, with reliable shelter in almost any weather.

Anchored under Chateau Costáeres at Ploumanac'h

L'Anse de Launay: This attractive bay lies between Pointe de la Trinité and Pointe de l'Arcouest, a little way N of the Anse de Paimpol. You can approach from the S via the Anse de Paimpol or from the N via Bréhat Roads and the Chenal de la Trinité. Coming from the S, follow the directions for the Chenal de la Trinité, but make for a position about a cable SE of Pointe de l'Arcouest once Les Fillettes S-cardinal beacon is within ¼ mile bearing N by W. Anchor clear of the local moorings and crab-pot buoys. Coming from the N, enter Chenal de la Trinité 1½ cables E of Les Piliers N-cardinal

beacon and follow the directions as far as Pointe d l'Arcouest.

L'Anse de Launay is best between neaps and springs in gentle westerly weather, although the off-lying rocks and the S shore of the Anse de Paimpol provide reasonable shelter from between S and SE. Only stay overnight if you are sure of the forecast, because it's difficult to leave in either direction after dark.

La Chambre: This charming anchorage off the SE corner of Ile de Bréhat is protected from between W through N to NE. Entry is

straightforward from Bréhat Roads, leaving three red spar beacons to port and a green spar beacon to starboard. If approaching from the E, pass well S of the S-cardinal beacon which stands about a cable S of Ile Logodec. Also keep clear of a long line of yellow floats marking an area of mussel beds to the E of this beacon.

Neaps are preferable for an overnight stay, because you can then stay afloat tucked well into the anchorage with maximum shelter from both wind and swell. At springs in calm weather, bilge-keelers can take the ground

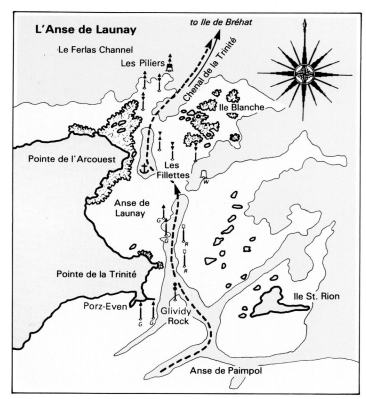

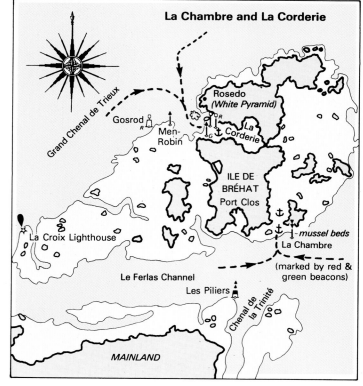

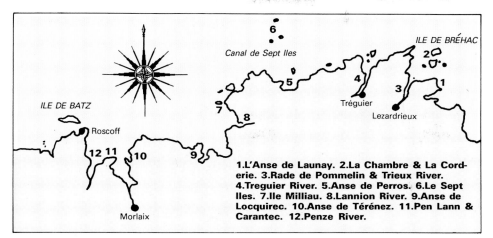

1.L'Anse de Launay. 2.La Chambre & La Corderie. 3.Rade de Pommelin & Trieux River. 4.Treguier River. 5.Anse de Perros. 6.Le Sept Iles. 7.Ile Milliau. 8.Lannion River. 9.Anse de Locquirec. 10.Anse de Térénez. 11.Pen Lann & Carantec. 12.Penze River.

just S of the local moorings. The landing slip on the W side of La Chambre is about 15 minutes pleasant stroll from the village of Le Bourg.

La Corderie: This fascinating inlet on the W side of Ile de Bréhat dries at springs, but the neap anchorage near the entrance is sheltered from SW through S to NE. Moderate westerlies present no real problem, since there's only a limited fetch across the estuary, but north-westerlies and northerlies can send

in a swell above half-tide. Approach from the Grand Chenal de Trieux by first making a position 200-250 metres due W of the Rosédo white pyramid daymark. Then head S for ¼ mile, between Men-Robin green spar beacon and Kervarec Rock. Once past Kervarec, turn ESE to enter La Corderie between two red spars and a green spar.

At springs, keel boats must fetch up just inside the outer beacons, but at neaps you can lie further in, towards or just beyond the next green. Bilge-keelers or boats with legs can

take the ground on firm sand right in the NE corner of La Corderie, one of the most secluded spots on the North Brittany coast.

Trieux River: Many yachtsmen visit the marina at Lézardrieux each season, but the river itself offers a number of quiet, sheltered anchorages in idyllic surroundings. There's a good spot off the W bank, 1-2 cables downstream from Perdrix light and inside or outside the local moorings depending on your draught. In the upper reaches of the Trieux, about 5 miles above Lézardrieux, you can stay afloat in a pool close off the W bank under the Château de la Roche-Jagu. To reach this anchorage, leave Lézardrieux about 1½ hours before HW.

Rade de Pommelin: This seemingly rather open roadstead lies on the W side of the Trieux estuary, to the WNW of Moguedhier green buoy. However, there's reasonable shelter here in moderate westerly weather, with good holding in sand and mud. Coming up the Grand Chenal, you simply bear to starboard about ¼ mile before Moguedhier green buoy, pass a cable to the N of the N-cardinal beacon which stands a little NW of Moguedhier, and anchor somewhere between Guazec Guen red spar

Tréguier

beacon and Hole Vras green spar beacon.

Tréguier River: There are various good anchorages in the lower reaches of the river if you don't want to go all the way up to the marina. In westerlies, you can anchor 3-4 cables SE of Ile Loaven, on the W side of the channel between the first two red buoys. Further upstream is a sheltered spot off the W bank between No 1 green conical buoy and Roche Don green spar beacon.

La Roche Jaune is a pleasant village on the W side of the Tréguier River, 1½ miles above the first red buoy. You can anchor slightly downstream of Roche Jaune, clear of the local moorings, where there's good shelter in all but fresh NE winds. There's another spot about ½ mile upstream from Roche Jaune, between No 5 green buoy and No 6 red. You must stay near the middle of the channel here because the sides dry out to steep banks of mud.

A useful and attractive anchorage for deep draught yachts is in the bight of the river just below No 10 red buoy, opposite Pointe Ker an Trêz. Fetch up close under the wooded W shore, with the large chateau-like house bearing about 260°M.

Port Blanc: This small fishing village and resort huddles behind a cordon of rocks between Tréguier entrance and Perros, providing an interesting anchorage in quiet summer weather or in winds with any south in them. It really comes under the 'harbour' category and there are directions in any of the North Brittany pilots.

Anse de Perros: In settled weather, you can anchor overnight a mile or so seaward of Perros harbour entrance, 3-4 cables SE of Pointe du Château and ¼ mile W of Roc'h Hu de Perros red beacon tower. This spot is protected from the W through S to SE, although there's usually a slight swell about two hours either side of HW. The anchorage

practically dries at LAT, but most boats will stay afloat at MLWS.

Les Sept Iles: There's a fair weather anchorage in the bay formed by Ile aux Moines and Ile de Bono. Approach from the SSE within 4

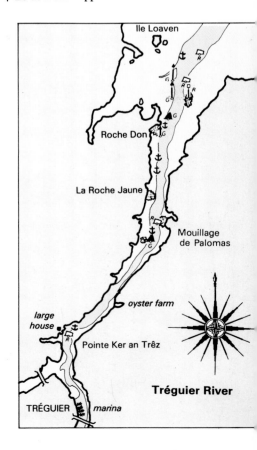

Rade de Pommelin and Trieux River

Tréguier River

Les Sept Iles

Anse de Perros

Ile Tomé
Pierre à Jean Rouzic
Roche Bernard
Pierre du Chenal
PERROS-GUIREC
Roc'h Hu de Perros
mooring buoys
local moorings
lock
marina
Gommonénou

Les Sept Iles

Ile de Malban
Ar Gazec
Ile Bono
Ile aux Moines
Les Dervinis

hrs of HW Perros, with Ile aux Moines lighthouse bearing 330°M. Alter to head for the W half of Ile de Bono when Les Dervinis S-cardinal buoy bears S of E. Anchor about 1½ cables off Ile aux Moines with the lighthouse bearing W mag. An overnight stay is not recommended unless the weather is quiet and settled.

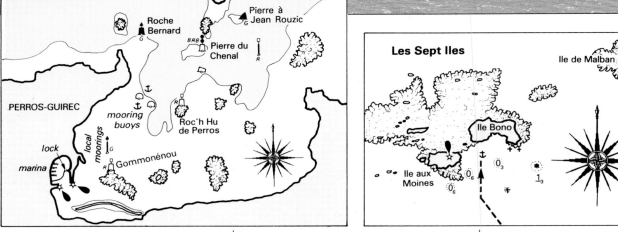

Ile Grande
Ile à Canton
osquet
Karreg Ar Merk
Ile Molène
Les Erviniou
r Gourédec
New marina under construction
Ile Milliau
TRÉBEURDEN
Les Roches
(2₈)
Ile Milliau

Ploumanac'h and Trégastel: I've placed these two under the 'harbour' category and their directions are well covered in the pilot books.

Ile Milliau: In the past, this picturesque spot was rarely visited by yachts, partly because it lies somewhat off the beaten track between the Tréguier and Morlaix rivers. Ile Milliau is only just an island, less than 2 cables offshore to the W of Trébeurden. The anchorage is close N of Milliau and ½ mile SE of Ile Molène. A new marina is being built in the bay off Trébeurden, just E of Ile Milliau, so the anchorage will become less secluded in the future.

The most straightforward approach is from

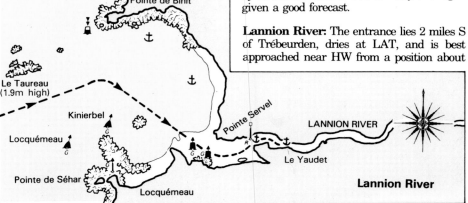

Pointe de Bihit
Le Taureau (1.9m high)
Kinierbel
Locquémeau
Pointe Servel
LANNION RIVER
Le Yaudet
Pointe de Séhar
Locquémeau
Lannion River

WSW, having first made a position 1¼ miles S of Le Crapaud W-cardinal buoy. From here, make good 076°M for not quite 3 miles towards the NW tip of Ile Milliau. The island is easy to identify with its two humps, but looks like a headland from a distance. As you draw near, pick up Ar Gourédec S-cardinal buoy, which marks the extremity of the dangers S of Ile Molène. When this buoy bears due N, alter course to pass midway between Ar Gourédec buoy and the NW tip of Milliau, then follow round the island into the anchorage. Fetch up with Les Erviniou W-cardinal beacon 2-3 cables away to the NW, or as far inshore to the SE as the tide allows.

This is really a fine weather anchorage, but is sheltered by Ile Molène from the NW, by the mainland from between NE and SE, and by Ile Milliau from S. You can stay overnight given a good forecast.

Lannion River: The entrance lies 2 miles S of Trébeurden, dries at LAT, and is best approached near HW from a position about

¼ mile S of Pointe de Bihit. From here, head SE to pass between Pointe Servel and Pointe du Dourven. Kinierbel green conical buoy is left ½ mile to starboard and two green beacon towers in the mouth of the river are left close to starboard. Keep the rear tower just open N of the front as you approach. Once past the second beacon, follow the curve of the S shore round to the NE and then leave a red spar beacon to port.

There's an anchorage in a pool just beyond this beacon off the N shore, and another a little further upstream off Le Yaudet. The river itself provides good shelter from all quarters, but entry or exit should never be attempted in fresh winds from between W and NW. The upper reaches dry, but it's interesting to make the four mile trip up to Lannion on the tide.

In quiet weather, or with the wind from between N through E to SSW, you can anchor in the bay to the N of the river mouth. The holding is only fair, mainly sand and rock, so you ought to lie to two anchors or plenty of chain if staying overnight.

Anse de Locquirec: This shallow sandy bay forms the estuary of Le Douron River. It lies between Pointe de Locquirec and Pointe de Plestin, 4 miles SW of the mouth of the Lannion River, and is sheltered from between W through S to SE. At neaps you can tuck well in under Pointe de Locquirec, a couple of

Anchorage and moorings off Trébeurden

cables E of the harbour breakwater, but at springs you must anchor midway between the tip of Pointe de Locquirec and Pointe de Plestin to stay afloat. The river flows into the S corner of the bay, but is only navigable by small boats; yachts should keep well clear of its mouth. It's best to approach Locquirec above half-tide, when two drying rocks in the offing — Roc'h Parou (dries 1.6m) and Roc'h Felestec (dries 1.3m) — will be well covered. Various drying rocks extend up to a mile N

and W of Pointe de Locquirec, so keep the bay well open as you come in.

Anse de Térénez: This narrow drying inlet lies on the E side of the Morlaix estuary and is approached via the Chenal de Tréguier above half-tide. Coming from seaward, follow the directions for the outer part of the Chenal de Tréguier, but alter course to the SE when Tourghi green beacon is 2 cables abeam to starboard. Steer towards a green spar beacon about ½ mile away, leaving it a cable to starboard, then head SSE towards Pointe de Térénez.

Near neaps, moderate draft boats can anchor and stay afloat close S of Pointe de

Rivière de Lannion

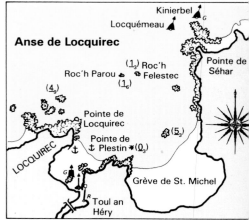

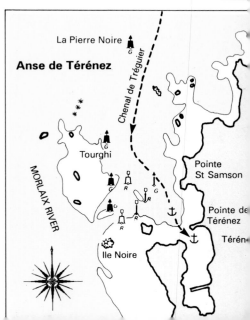

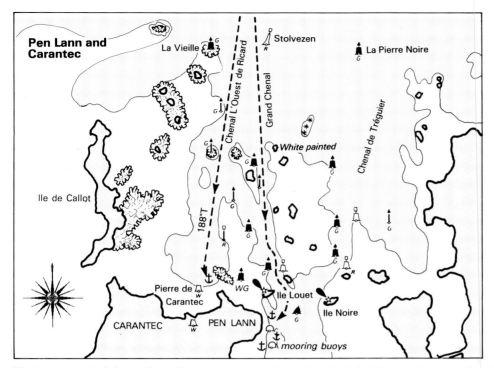

Pen Lann and Carantec

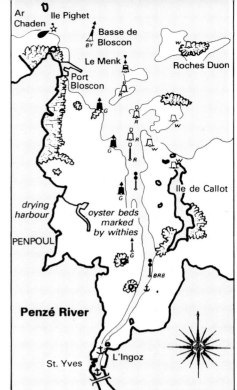

Penzé River

Térénez, protected from all winds except a fresh north-westerly. Bilge-keelers may edge further into the inlet and take the ground. At springs, keel boats will stay afloat about 3 cables NW of Pointe de Térénez.

Pen Lann: This is the usual passage anchorage for yachts waiting for the tide up to Morlaix, but it also makes a snug overnight berth unless the wind is fresh from the S. Protection from fresh onshore winds is provided by the natural breakwater of rocks and shoals in the outer part of the estuary.

Enter the Morlaix River, either via the Grand Chenal or the Chenal de Tréguier, and fetch up close E or SE of Pen Lann Point. You can either anchor or use one of the three secure visitors' moorings. In onshore winds, and near neaps, you will obtain greater shelter by edging further round to the S of Pen Lann.

Carantec: There's a fair-weather anchorage to the NW of Pen Lann, with Grand Cochon green and white beacon tower bearing due E true about 2 cables distant. Coming from

seaward, follow the directions for the Chenal Ouest de Ricard but continue along this line (188°T) towards the N side of the Carantec peninsula. As you draw inshore, the two white leading marks for the Chenal Ouest de Ricard should come into clear view. Follow their transit almost as far as you can, but edge to port a little before reaching the front mark — the white painted Pierre de Carantec. Anchor a cable NE of this rock, making sure that you don't get too close to the drying reef a cable WNW of Grand Cochon beacon.

This spot has about ½ metre at LAT, so it can be used by moderate draft yachts even at MLWS. However, quiet settled weather is needed, because the anchorage is much more open to swell than the inner part of the estuary at Pen Lann.

La Penzé River: The Penzé estuary opens into the W side of the bay of Morlaix and is navigable for about four miles as far as St Yves. The river is quiet and sheltered and there are various anchorages in or near the narrow deep-water channel. The most protected is right up at St Yves, a cable SW of l'Ingoz white beacon in 1½m MLWS. It's preferable to enter the estuary above half-tide, starting from 2 cables W of Le Menk W-cardinal beacon tower and following the red and green beacon towers southwards.

USEFUL ADMIRALTY CHARTS

No 3673 — Lézardrieux and Paimpol with approaches
No 3672 — Harbours on the NW coast of France
No 3669 — Anse de Kernic to Les Sept Iles
No 2745 — Approaches to Roscoff and Morlaix
No 3668 — Le Four to Anse de Kernic
No 1432 — Le Four to Ile Vierge

Carantec Ile Callot

Chapter 3
Ile de Batz to L'Aberildut

As you work westwards past Roscoff and Ile de Batz, the north coast of Brittany becomes more low-lying and rather tricky to identify from off-shore. It takes on a harder, more austere mood than hitherto, and there are plenty of drying rocks which don't appear until the ebb is well away. You can reckon a good 35 miles from the Morlaix estuary to L'Abervrac'h, a full tide under sail, and most yachts aim to make a quick passage between the two without lingering on the way. This doesn't seem, on the face of it, an area suitable for nudging into seclud-ed bays and inlets. Yet even this stretch of coast has a handful of natur-al havens where, given the right conditions and a favourable forecast, you can tuck close in and lie to your own ground-tackle undisturbed.

There are several attractive spots off the south-east side of Ile de Batz, in the narrow Chenal de Batz which only just seems to separate the island from the mainland. In fact the French have laid heavy-duty visitors' buoys in some of the positions where one used to lie at anchor. This is a pity in a way, since perfect seclusion is now that bit more elu-sive, but on the whole the moorings are a welcome addition; the tidal streams can be strong in the Chenal de Batz and there are various unpredictable eddies close inshore where, on a long scope near low water, you can find yourself swinging rather closer to dry land than intended.

The Chenal de Batz, usually called the Canal de l'Ile de Batz on English charts, is a fascinating narrow passage just over three miles from end to end. Most yachts use it as a short cut when coasting, rather than make a long detour round the rocky dangers seaward of Ile de Batz. The channel looks intricate in prospect, but is well marked and fairly straightforward once you get going. The east end is shallow, with soundings down to half a metre at LAT, so you really need a couple of hours' rise of tide at springs. This is usually no problem when carrying a fair stream in either direction between the Morlaix estuary and L'Abervrac'h, but needs watching if you are making shorter local hops between anchorages.

The western end of the Chenal de Batz, near Basse Plate north-car-dinal beacon tower, passes about 1½ miles off the mainland to clear a wide area of dangers extending well offshore. This plateau needs to be skirted by a safe margin as you curve round to the south-west to enter the bay which has Ile de Siec on its north side and tiny Moguériec har-bour in its south-west corner. The anchorages in this bay are attractive and secluded places to lie for a day or two, but they are also useful pas-sage stops, cutting the distance along the coast to L'Abervrac'h entrance to something like 25 miles. This leg makes a comfortable one-tide pas-sage which you can usually sail, even in a head-wind, without much risk of picking up a foul stream before you arrive.

The anchorage off Ile de Siec, between Querelevran rock and the west end of the island, is a good spot in easterlies, especially near neaps. *Stormalong* once lay here for several days late in the season while a near-gale from more or less due east raged in the English Channel. We had beat along from L'Abervrac'h in a nasty steep chop while the wind was freshening, running out of fair tide before reaching the Chenal de Batz and grateful for the lee of Ile de Siec and its nearby crook of main-land. I had intended to slip round to Morlaix on the next tide, but the wind became so chill and malevolent that we laid out a second anchor, lit the cabin stove and settled down to wait, reading good books between long, leisurely meals. Each afternoon we would row across to the island for a bracing walk to work up an appetite for dinner.

You can land with the dinghy at an old stone jetty just north-east of the anchorage, opposite the prominent wartime ruins of a house at the west tip of Ile de Siec. The island has a small-holding and one or two holiday cottages, but is otherwise uninhabited. At low water, you can walk across a sand-spit causeway to the mainland and the small ham-let of Dossen. An alternative anchorage in winds with any south in them is off the entrance to Moguériec, on the south side of the bay. This is a snug spot in offshore weather, with the advantages of a couple of shops and a congenial hôtel-restaurant ashore. In season, you can enjoy a shower at the camp-site just inland from the south quay.

Some 10 miles west of Moguériec and Ile de Siec, on the west side of the shallow Anse de Kernic, is the small natural harbour of Pontusval. This U-shaped inlet in the low-lying coast is entered from northward between two wide areas of drying rocks which straggle out from each side of the mouth. These rocks help protect the inlet from swell so that, in moderate or offshore weather, a yacht can anchor and stay afloat in the narrow approach channel to the drying part of the harbour.

When pressed for time on the way up-Channel, we have sometimes used Pontusval after coming up through the Chenal du Four early on the tide and made sufficiently good progress round the coast to carry the east-going stream beyond L'Abervrac'h. By starting next day from Pontusval on the last of the west-going stream, you can aim to get through the Chenal de Batz and along the coast as far as Ploumanac'h before the tide turns foul again.

The North Brittany coast around Pontusval often feels rather hostile and one can be reluctant to turn shorewards to find the narrow entrance. However, the approach is actually quite simple, so long as you start from the Pontusval east-cardinal buoy, moored just opposite the entrance not quite a mile offshore. The tall radio aerial a couple of miles inland is a useful mark when trying to locate this buoy.

Heading west towards L'Abervrac'h, you would normally pass two miles north of the tall lighthouse on Ile Vierge, on the leg between Lizen Ven west-cardinal buoy and a turning waypoint a mile or so north of Le Libenter west-cardinal buoy at the entrance to the estuary. However, on a quiet day when the tide is right, an intrepid navigator can edge in close to Ile Vierge from Lizen Ven buoy, leave the west end of the island close to port, and feel his way gently south-east between the reefs into a narrow sandy inlet known as Portz Malo. This natural drying harbour is used by a few local fishing and seaweed-gathering boats and offers a splendid hideaway for a yacht with bilge-keels. You can lie here in per-fect solitude in the lee of Ile Vénan, less than two miles from the marina at L'Abervrac'h and saving in dues each night the cost of a good French meal.

You need to keep an eye on the forecast of course, but Portz Malo is worth the slight stress of pilotage involved in getting in. I was last there in a Westerly Konsort, the weather set fair for a while with a light breeze from the south-west. It was somewhat eerie to be dried out on firm sand at midnight a mile inside Ile Vierge, watching its single pow-erful beam sweep this potentially treacherous corner of North Brittany. We weren't disturbed by anyone until late morning, when a Frenchman staying on holiday nearby knocked diffidently on the hull and presented us with a bag of freshly gathered mussels, just in time for lunch.

On then to the real heart of the Côte des Abers — L'Abervrac'h, L'Aberbenoit, L'Aberildut — and a selection of rarely visited, off-beat anchorages in the northern approaches to the Chenal du Four. This north-west corner of Brittany can be an absorbing cruising area in its own right, and yet most yachts pass through quickly, perhaps calling at L'Abervrac'h for a night before pressing on down through the Chenal du Four bound for Camaret, the Raz de Sein and the Biscay coast.

The Chenal du Four is an important tidal gate for this corner and you need to carry a fair stream when cruising anywhere between L'Abervrac'h and Pointe de St Mathieu, where the Chenal du Four joins the Brest estuary. Yachts heading south from L'Abervrac'h right through the Four would normally aim to stem the last of the east-going tide, leaving L'Abervrac'h about an hour before local high water. There is more flexibility, however, if you are making shorter hops between anchorages.

A fresh wind over tide kicks up a steep chop in the southern, shal-lowest part of the Chenal du Four. Poor visibility is common in the whole area, although the buoyage is excellent and it's usually not diffi-cult to pick your way around even in quite murky conditions. The real potential menace is heavy north-westerly swell, especially at the north end of the Chenal du Four, which can soon make some of the smaller anchorages untenable.

L'Abervrac'h

1. Ile de Batz. 2. Ile de Siec and Moguériec. 3. Pontusval. 4. Portz Malo - Ile Vierge. 5. L'Abervrac'h River. 6. L'Aberbenoit. 7. Portsall. 8. Argenton. 9. Melon. 10. L'Aberildut

Ile de Batz: There are several possible anchorages in the Canal de l'Ile de Batz, the narrow sound which separates the island from the Brittany mainland. Working from the E, the first spot is between Ile Pighet white beacon and Duslen S-cardinal beacon tower, but closer to Ile Pighet than Duslen to avoid the rock awash on the direct line between the two. This anchorage is best at neaps because you can tuck in northwards out of the strong tidal stream. Reasonable shelter from between NW and SW.*

Further into the sound, you can fetch up 1½-2 cables E of the S-cardinal spar beacon which marks the S extremity of the long LW landing slip at Portz Kernoch. At neaps you can edge inshore to find quieter water, but make sure that the landing slip beacon is bearing no less than 265°M as there are ledges of drying rocks to the N of this line. There's also an anchorage just off Portz Kernoch entrance, within a cable WSW of Malvoch S-cardinal beacon tower. Both these spots are sheltered in any northerly winds.*

*Moorings buoys for visitors have recently been laid in both these locations. Editor.

At neaps, moderate draft yachts can stay afloat in Portz Kernoch itself, opposite the entrance and about half-way along the LW landing slip. Ile de Batz is picturesque and well worth an expedition ashore.

Ile de Siec and Moguériec: Ile de Siec lies very close to the North Brittany coast, a little over 2 miles SSW of the W entrance to the Canal de l'Ile de Batz. Numerous drying rocks extend up to 1½ miles offshore between Roscoff and Ile de Siec, but there's an interesting deep-water anchorage about a cable SW of the W tip of Ile de Siec, sheltered in moderate weather from between NE through E to S.

Approach from the NNW within 2 hours of HW, from a position 2¼ miles due W of Basse Plate N-cardinal beacon tower. Make good

Ile de Batz

Aerial photographs courtesy of E. Guillemot/Blue Sky.

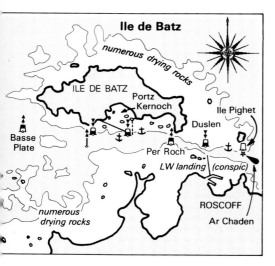

Ile de Batz

numerous drying rocks

ILE DE BATZ

Portz Kernoch

Basse Plate

Ile Pighet

Duslen

Per Roch

LW landing (conspic)

ROSCOFF

Ar Chaden

numerous drying rocks

162°T towards Moguériec pierhead (3 miles away), aiming to pass ¼ mile W of Golchedec — the islet close off the W tip of Ile de Siec. There are dangers to the W of this line, of which the most significant is Méan Névez (dries 3.3m). Once the W tip of Ile de Siec bears N of E, come to port and fetch up in the bay formed by Golchedec, Ile de Siec and Querelevran rock. At neaps, in quiet weather, you can edge further E between Ile de Siec and Querelevran, but be sure to anchor clear of the rocky ledges on either hand.

The small fishing village of Moguériec lies at the mouth of the Rivière du Guillec, a mile S by W from Ile de Siec. A stone pier protects its local moorings from the N. At neaps, in quiet or offshore weather, you can anchor and stay afloat 2 cables NNE of Moguériec pierhead.

Pontusval: This tiny natural harbour, hemmed in by rocks, lies 12 miles WSW along the coast from l'Ile de Batz and about 10 miles ENE from Ile Vierge lighthouse. Few yachts call at Pontusval, perhaps because the coastline either side often looks rather inhospitable. However, the approach is fairly straightforward (in daylight and preferably above half-tide) given reasonable visibi-

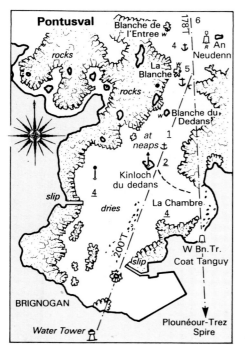

Pontusval

rocks

Blanche de l'Entree

An Neudenn

La Blanche

rocks

Blanche du Dedans

at neaps

Kinloch du dedans

slip

dries

La Chambre

W Bn.Tr. Coat Tanguy

slip

BRIGNOGAN

Water Tower

Plounéour-Trez Spire

Pt de Bloscon, Roscoff

lity, light or offshore winds, and an absence of swell.

The most useful landmarks are Pointe de Beg Pol lighthouse, a mile W of the entrance, and a tall radio mast a couple of miles inland

from the lighthouse. You will find a surfeit of water towers, so be careful about using these for establishing your position. The pilot books give various transits, but the easiest guide is to reach Pontusval E-cardinal buoy first and

Mogueriec

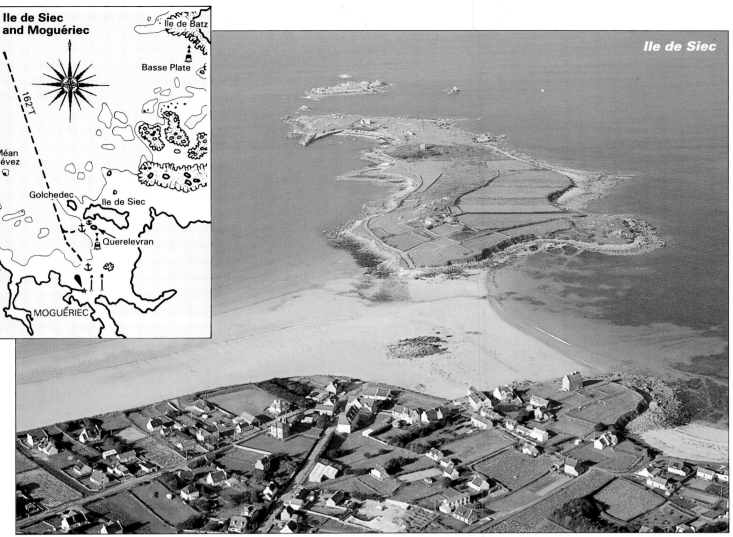

Ile de Siec and Moguériec

Ile de Siec

L'Abervrac'h

then make good 178°T towards the entrance (less than a mile away), allowing for the cross-tide which you assessed at the buoy.

On entry, leave Pecher green buoy to starboard, An Neudenn red beacon tower to port, and three white-painted rocks to starboard. At springs, keel boats should fetch up opposite the second white rock; at neaps you can venture past the third white rock, anchoring in mid-channel between this and Kinloc'h du Dédans spar beacon. Pontusval provides good shelter in any winds from the S.

Portz Malo (Ile Vierge): A fascinating spot for bilge-keelers, this narrow sandy inlet lies amongst the various rocks and islets between Ile Vierge and the mainland. It should only be visited in quiet settled weather and preferably near neaps, but the approach is easier than you might imagine, starting from a position ¾ mile NW of Ile Vierge light-house. You need to identify Ile Valan, a small island lying 2 cables S of the W tip of Ile Vierge; Ile Valan has a detached rock, 15m high, close NW of it. Also identify Lanvaon lighthouse, a white square tower a couple of miles inland behind Ile Vierge to the SE. Lanvaon normally forms the rear leading mark for the Grand Chenal de l'Abervrac'h.

Bring Ile Valan open its own width to the W of Lanvaon lighthouse, with the latter bearing 137°T, and steer in between Ile Vierge and Ile Valan on this transit. Continue towards Lanvaon until Ile Valan is abeam about 80 metres to starboard and then come to port a shade so as to leave Ile Vénan (19m

L'Aberbenoît

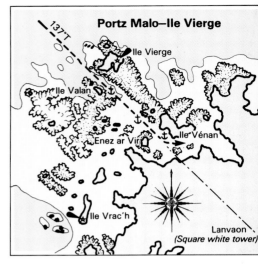
Portz Malo—Ile Vierge

137°T
Ile Vierge
Ile Valan
Ile Vénan
Enez ar Vir
Ile Vrac'h
Lanvaon
(Square white tower)

high) not quite 100 metres to port and the much smaller Enez ar Vir (9m high) about a cable to starboard.

Fetch up off the S side of Ile Vénan, where the sandy channel dries between 3½ and 5 metres LAT. There are one or two patches of rock and weed which need to be avoided as you take the ground. Portz Malo is sheltered in any winds from the S.

L'Abervrac'h Estuary: Of the many yachts that visit L'Abervrac'h each season, the majority are hurrying either home or south and simply stay overnight at the small marina at La Palue or lie to one of the club moorings. However, there are one or two anchorages which allow you to get away from the madding crowd.

In settled weather, especially from the S, you can fetch up in the outer part of the estuary, 1½-2 cables ESE of Ile de la Croix and just about a cable SSW of Basse de la Croix green conical buoy. Approach Ile de la Croix from the ESE and anchor well clear of a small rock (dries 3.4m) which lies just over a cable E of the N end of Ile de la Croix. Don't stray too far S towards the rocky patches lurking up to ¼ mile N of Penn Enez.

There are several sheltered anchorages above Pointe Cameuleut, in the upper reaches of the river, but you must keep clear of local moorings and the various mussel beds along the foreshore; the latter are marked by withies. There is a good spot ½ mile or so above Pointe Cameuleut off the S bank, but it's really a question of finding swinging room on the day. The pool up at Paluden provides a pleasant anchorage, protected from all

Ile Vierge

quarters and with 4ft LAT about 100yds SE of the quay. There's a good family restaurant nearby and the small town of Lannilis is just over a mile's walk.

L'Aberbenoit: This attractive unspoilt estuary lies only a couple of miles SSE of Le Libenter whistle buoy, but most yachts pass it by in favour of L'Abervrac'h. Entry is possible at any state of tide, but only in daylight and reasonable visibility. Avoid L'Aberbenoit in heavy swell or in strong W or NW winds. From Le Libenter find La Petite Fourche W-cardinal buoy, 6 cables to the SSW, then follow the lateral buoys S and SE towards the narrow entrance. Once you are in the river, L'Aberbenoit offers an excellent anchorage sheltered from all quarters.

In quiet or offshore weather you can anchor off the beach, just inside the entrance on the W side. Otherwise, continue ½ mile further up to Le Passage, anchoring in midstream clear of the local moorings, just below or just above Pointe du Passage and its landing slip. Don't stray more than ¼ mile

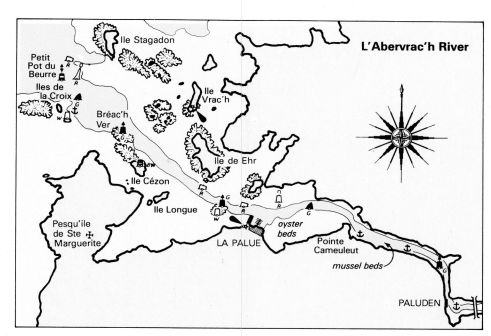

above Le Passage, where the river starts to shoal very quickly.

Portsall: Most yachts tend to hurry past Portsall, on this rocky NW corner of Brittany where the tanker *Amoco Cadiz* came to grief; she is still there, surrounded by an 'exclusion zone'. There are, however, various anchorages off Portsall harbour which are fine in quiet weather or with the wind from between S through SE to E. Strangers should approach from the W via the Chenal de Men Glas, having first made a position with Le Four lighthouse bearing about 210°M distant 2½ miles. Slack water is preferable (either HW or LW Brest). Coming from the Chenal du Four, be sure to stay well outside Roches d'Argenton, a long string of drying dangers extending 2½ miles NE of Le Four lighthouse. Coming from L'Abervrac'h or L'Aberbenoit, give a wide berth to Roches de Portsall, just as if you were southbound for the Chenal du Four.

Enter Portsall outer anchorage heading a shade N of E leaving Bosven Aval rock (4.9m high) to port, Men ar Pic green beacon tower to starboard, and Ile Verte south rock (4.9m high) to port. Near LW avoid Basse Idic (awash at LAT 2 cables E

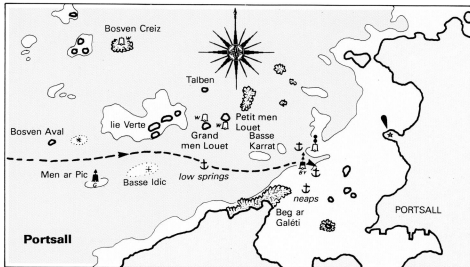

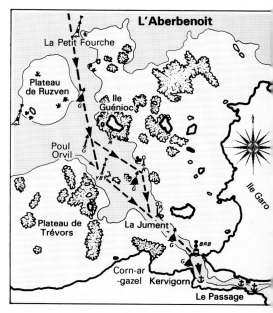

27

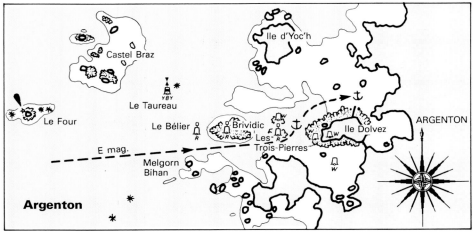

Argenton

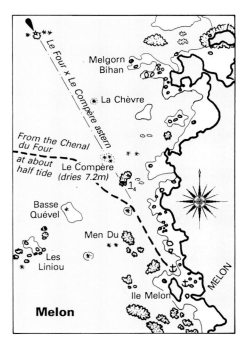

Melon

by N from Men ar Pic) and fetch up 1-1½ cables S of Grand Men Louet islet (11m high). This outer anchorage is easy to leave at night, using the white sector of Portsall light (Oc3+1, WRG,12s). With sufficient rise of tide you can continue just beyond Basse Karrat (0.1m LAT) to anchor 100m W of Besquel BRB beacon tower or 60m SE of La Pendante N-cardinal beacon tower. Near neaps you will find better shelter from swell by edging closer to Portsall harbour and anchoring 100m S of La Pendante. Use Admiralty Chart No 1432.

Argenton: This interesting anchorage lies 1½ miles E of Le Four lighthouse, but should only be visited in light or easterly winds in the absence of swell. From a position ¼ mile S of Le Four, make good due E mag towards the entrance, aiming to pass midway between Le Bélier red beacon, left to port, and Melgorn Bihan rock (10m high), left to starboard. Now pick up the leading marks — the front mark a dumpy white beacon tower in front of Ile Dolvez and the rear mark a white pyramid on the island itself. Keep these two exactly in transit bearing 083°T, leaving Brividic and Les Trois Pierres red beacon towers to port. Take special care to avoid the drying rocks extending ESE from Brividic.

At ordinary springs, moderate draft yachts will stay afloat in the area between Les Trois Pierres and the front leading mark, or further N with Men Hir white beacon tower in line with Le Four. At neaps, shallow draught boats will find better shelter in the sandy bay NNE of Ile Dolvez. Use Admiralty Chart No 3345.

Melon: Two miles S of the entrance to Argenton, this small natural drying harbour is protected from the W by Ile Melon. In quiet weather, approach at half-tide from the NNW, having passed between Les Liniou and Le Four lighthouse and then having also kept 2 cables W of Le Compère rock (dries 7.2m). Le Four in transit with Le Compère astern leads into the outer anchorage a cable N of Ile Melon. Shallow draft boats can anchor E of Ile Melon at neaps.

L'Aberildut: This natural harbour is well covered by the pilot books, but it's worth remembering that the anchorage outside the bar is accessible at all states of tide and offers a snug overnight berth in easterlies, provided there's no onshore swell. The approach is relatively straightforward from the Chenal du Four, leaving Pierre de Laber green beacon to starboard, Le Lieu red beacon tower to port, then keeping well S of the drying rocks which lie between Le Lieu and the N side of the river entrance. Anchor as near to the entrance as soundings permit and be sure to show a riding light at night. The best spot near neaps is a cable due W of the S head of the entrance, where the sandy bottom dries 1½m at LAT. Use Admiralty Chart No 3345. ●

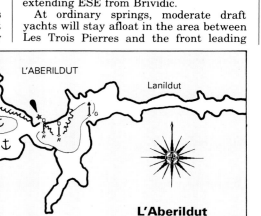

L'Aberildut

USEFUL ADMIRALTY CHARTS

No 3673 — Lézardrieux and Paimpol with approaches
No 3672 — Harbours on the NW coast of France
No 3669 — Anse de Kernic to Les Sept Iles
No 2745 — Approaches to Roscoff and Morlaix
No 3668 — Le Four to Anse de Kernic
No 1432 — Le Four to Ile Vierge
No 3345 — Chenal du Four

L'Aberildut

Chapter 4
Chenal du Four to the Raz de Sein

The far west of Finistère has a character all of its own. Hardly less rugged than the Côtes du Nord, considering the maze of reefs and islands lurking seaward of the Chenal du Four, and the rather sinister Chaussée de Sein further south, it nevertheless has more mainland coastline which is navigationally straightforward. Between Le Four and the Raz, there's more scope for edging inshore and dropping the hook than you'll find, for example, between Lézardrieux and L'Abervrac'h.

This is partly because of some long stretches of steep-to cliffs and bays which are more or less uncluttered by off-lying rocks. But you also have two large inlets: L'Iroise, which leads to the Rade de Brest and the Elorn and Aulne estuaries; and, further south, the attractive sweep of the Bay of Douarnenez.

In this chapter, starting with Portz Paul, I'll be looking at a few anchorages just off the Chenal du Four before striking offshore for Ushant, Ile de Molène and Ile de Quéménès. Then inland to the Rade de Brest and some peaceful river hideaways before cutting round the corner, via the Chenal de Toulinguet, into the Bay of Douarnenez. We fetch up in the Baie des Trépassés, just north of the Raz de Sein.

The islands which lie seaward of the Chenal du Four are often appreciated, perhaps unknowingly, for the protection they give from swell, yet they are rarely visited by yachts from the UK. This has partly to do with the somewhat forbidding atmosphere surrounding this north-west corner of Brittany, with its powerful tides and exposed position facing the Atlantic; it also has to do with timing and the fact that most yachts using the Chenal du Four are cruising to a tight schedule — either trying to get well south at the start of a Biscay cruise, or hurrying home again.

There is no doubt that, having reached the outer marks for the Chenal du Four, it takes a certain effort of will to direct your course out to the west, towards the islands of Ushant, Molène and Quéménès. Having done it once, though, you'll find that the solitude of the island anchorages will draw you offshore time and again when cruising past this area.

Ushant — Ile d'Ouessant in French — is by far the largest of the Finistère islands, some four and a half miles long by two miles wide. As North Brittany goes, the Ushant coast is fairly steep-to, except off its south-west corner inside La Jument lighthouse, and on the north side where the Chaussée de Keller rocks straggle a good three quarters of a mile WNW of Ile de Keller. Elsewhere, you will stay in safe water by keeping at least half a mile seaward of the nearest visible offlying rock.

Ushant has two main harbours which are also useful anchorages: Lampaul, at the head of the long bay on the south-west side of the island; and Le Stiff, the landing place on the east side which is normally used by the mainland ferries and tourist vedettes. Le Stiff is a relatively easy point of arrival for yachts coming across from the north end of the Chenal du Four, and is reasonably protected with the wind in the west. It's a convenient anchorage to make for if visiting Ushant for the first time, and the tall radar control tower on the north side of the bay is an unmistakeable landmark.

However, Lampaul is rather more attractive than Le Stiff and handy for the island's shops and hôtel-restaurants. It is also more sheltered than you might think from the chart since, at least in moderate weather, the long bay of Lampaul seems to filter out a good deal of any westerly swell. Some visitors' moorings have recently been laid at the head of the bay opposite the lifeboat slip, although there is still room to anchor.

Ashore, Ushant is harsh and windswept, well dotted with houses but practically treeless. There are some dramatic coastal views, especially on the north side, and it's interesting to walk down to Créac'h lighthouse, one of the most powerful in Europe. From here, on a clear day, you can see the steady procession of ships entering and leaving the Channel via the Ushant traffic lanes.

Between Ushant and the south end of the Chenal du Four is a complex string of reefs and small, low-lying islands. Much of this area is tricky to navigate without local knowledge, but I have included two of the most accessible anchorages — off Ile de Molène and Ile de Quéménès. Molène lies about five miles seaward of the Chenal du Four, although the safest approach for strangers is from the north, leaving Plateau de la Helle to the east. The tidal streams near the island are not so savage as those around Ushant, and the waters are partly protected from swell by the surrounding reefs. Molène is only just over half a mile long, but the village on its east side is quite densely packed.

Ile de Quéménès is a couple of miles south-east of Molène, about the same length but much narrower and lying east-west. It has a few cottages, mainly towards its west end, but the east end near the anchorage and landing slip is more or less deserted. The anchorage is approached from the south and is well protected in moderate westerly weather, especially as the tide falls away and the rocky plateau to the north of Quéménès uncovers.

Back on the mainland, the sheltered Rade de Brest, the estuaries of the Elorn and the Aulne, and the higher reaches of these two rivers, offer a delightful cruising ground with enough rural anchorages to keep a relaxed crew going for a month. This is an ideal area for gentle family pottering, especially when the weather at sea is cutting up rough. It also tends to be fairly uncrowded, since the detour involved in entering the Rade de Brest discourages many crews on passage, who tend to pass by outside the entrance, heading purposefully north or south. You have the facilities of the Anse de Moulin Blanc marina for topping up with fuel, water and stores, and then you can lose yourself in quiet waters, tucked away in creeks and inlets.

In a similar way, the spectacular stretch of coastline between Camaret and the Raz de Sein is often taken for granted by crews hurrying past to a schedule. Yet there are several good anchorages to escape to hereabouts, either outside or inside the Bay of Douarnenez, according to wind and weather. The tides in this area are fairly weak, compared with those in the Chenal du Four to the north and the Raz de Sein to the south. The pilotage is generally straightforward, especially in the Bay of Douarnenez, although you have to be a bit careful about the off-lying dangers when rounding Cap de la Chèvre.

Estuary of the Rivière de Pouldavid at Douarnenez

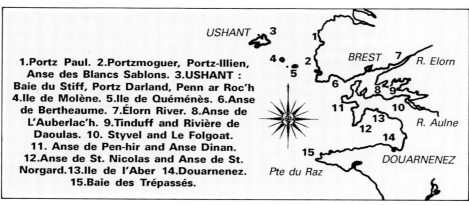

1.Portz Paul. 2.Portzmoguer, Portz-Illien, Anse des Blancs Sablons. 3.USHANT : Baie du Stiff, Portz Darland, Penn ar Roc'h 4.Ile de Molène. 5.Ile de Quéménès. 6.Anse de Bertheaume. 7.Élorn River. 8.Anse de L'Auberlac'h. 9.Tinduff and Rivière de Daoulas. 10. Styvel and Le Folgoat. 11. Anse de Pen-hir and Anse Dinan. 12.Anse de St. Nicolas and Anse de St. Norgard.13.Ile de l'Aber 14.Douarnenez. 15.Baie des Trépassés.

Portz Paul: This small drying harbour lies not quite 2 miles SSW of L'Aberildut and offers an outer anchorage in quiet weather or easterlies provided there's no swell. The key mark is the islet of Grande Fourche

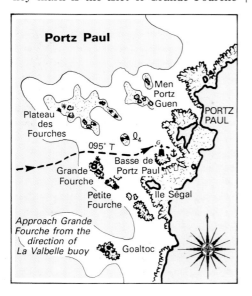

Portz Paul

(13m high) which lies 1¼ miles E of La Valbelle buoy. Approach Grande Fourche above half-tide from the direction of La Valbelle, to be sure of avoiding the Plateau des Fourches, a dangerous area of drying rocks ¼ mile N of Grande Fourche. Aim to pass 1-1½ cables N of Grande Fourche (and no further), with Basse de Portz Paul green beacon tower bearing 095°T dead ahead. Round this beacon tower by a cable and fetch up a cable ENE of it. Boats which can take the ground will be able to carry on into the harbour and dry out on firm sand clear of the local moorings.

Anse de Portzmoguer: An attractive bay off the Chenal du Four, ¾ mile SE of Pointe de Corsen. It provides good shelter from N through E to SE and is straightforward to enter by day. When approaching from the S though, be sure to avoid Basse Jaune, a ledge of drying rocks extending nearly ¼ mile NW of Pointe du Brenterc'h. There are also numerous crab-pot floats in the area. Portzmoguer has a good many small boat moorings and it's usually best to anchor outside them, close under the low headland on the NW side of the bay. This anchorage

is easy to leave at night, provided you keep a sharp lookout for pot floats.

Portz Illien: A small bay ½ mile SSE of Pointe de Brenterc'h, on the NE side of the Anse des Blancs Sablons. Although sheltered from N through E to SE, it's not quite so easy to enter as Portzmoguer. An isolated rock (drying 2.7m) lies just over a cable NW of the S head of the entrance and a ledge of drying rocks extending over a cable W and 100m S of the N head. The easiest time to enter is near low water, when you can leave the rocks off the N side of the entrance close to port and be sure of leaving the isolated rock well to starboard.

Anse des Blancs Sablons: A wide sandy bay on the N side of Presqu'île de Kermorvan. There's a useful anchorage in the SW corner, sheltered from SW through S to SE. The approach is straightforward, but give a good berth to L'Illette when the ebb is setting strongly onto it. Use Admiralty Chart No 3345.

Ushant: This rather forbidding but atmospheric island is best visited at neaps in

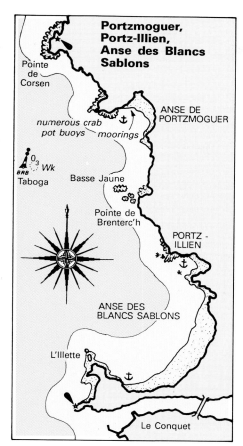

Portzmoguer, Portz-Illien, Anse des Blancs Sablons

Pointe de Corsen

ANSE DE PORTZMOGUER

numerous crab pot buoys

moorings

O₃ Wk
BRB
Taboga

Basse Jaune

Pointe de Brenterc'h

PORTZ-ILLIEN

ANSE DES BLANCS SABLONS

L'Illette

Le Conquet

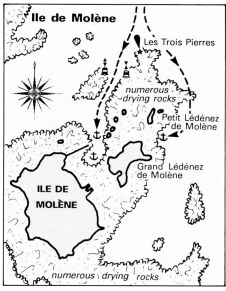

Ile de Molène

Les Trois Pierres

numerous drying rocks

Petit Lédénez de Molène

Grand Lédénez de Molène

ILE DE MOLÈNE

numerous drying rocks

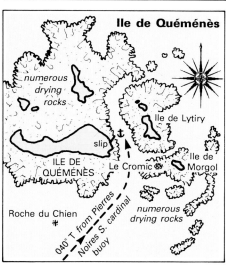

Ile de Quéménès

numerous drying rocks

Ile de Lytiry

slip

ILE DE QUÉMÉNÈS

Le Cromic

Ile de Morgol

Roche du Chien

numerous drying rocks

040° T from Pierres Noires S. cardinal buoy

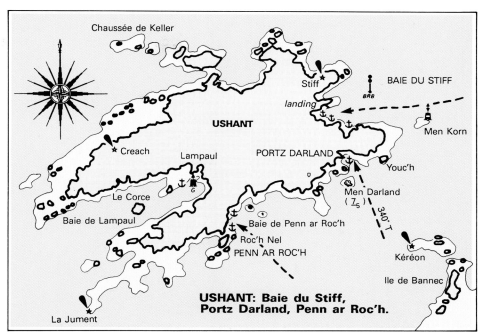

Chaussée de Keller

Stiff

BAIE DU STIFF
BRB

landing

Men Korn

USHANT

Creach

Lampaul

PORTZ DARLAND

Youc'h

Le Corce

G

Men Darland
(Z₅)

Baie de Lampaul

Baie de Penn ar Roc'h

Roc'h Nel

PENN AR ROC'H

340° T

Kéréon

Ile de Bannec

USHANT: Baie du Stiff, Portz Darland, Penn ar Roc'h.

La Jument

Ile de Molène

Aerial Photographs by E. Guillemot/Blue Sky

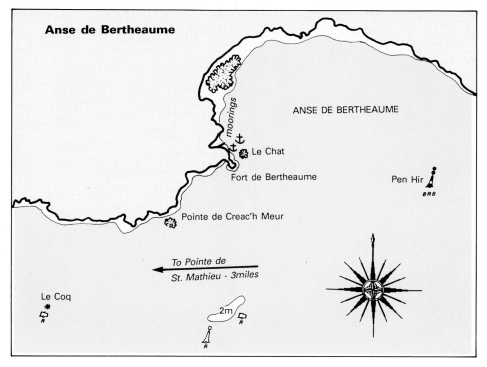

Anse de Bertheaume

moorings

ANSE DE BERTHEAUME

Le Chat

Fort de Bertheaume

Pen Hir
BRB

Pointe de Creac'h Meur

To Pointe de St. Mathieu - 3miles

Le Coq

2m

R

R

R

quiet weather and good visibility. There are visitors' moorings at the main harbour of Lampaul, on the SW side of Ushant, and various anchorages in the Baie de Lampaul depending on wind direction. On the E coast of the island, the Baie du Stiff offers reasonable shelter in westerlies and makes a fairly straightforward landfall from the N end of the Chenal du Four. It's usually best to tuck into one of the three smaller inlets within the Baie du Stiff — Portz Liboudou, Portz an Dour or Portz Aheac'h — so you are clear of the mainland ferry.

Portz Darland, in the SE corner of the island, is protected in north-westerlies. Approach from the SSE, preferably at LW when the various drying rocks on either hand are well exposed. From at least ½ mile offshore, identify the stone jetty on the W side of Portz Darland and the sandy beach just E of the jetty. Bring Le Stiff lighthouse into line with the E end of the beach bearing 340°T and close the shore on this transit leaving Men Darland rock (drying 7.5m) and Fret Kas rocks (drying 5.8m) each a cable to port. Anchor off the jetty, as close to the beach as your draught allows. About 1½ miles SW of Portz Darland is the Baie de Penn ar Roc'h, which has anchorages on its W side about a cable N of Roc'h Nel (10m high) or further N in the Anse de Boug an Dour. Approach from SE near slack water, leaving Roc'h Nel a cable to port. The French SHOM Chart No 5567 is invaluable for Ushant.

Ile de Molène: This little-visited island lies between Ushant and Le Conquet in a somewhat formidable area of drying rocks and powerful tides. However, in quiet weather near neaps, the harbour is easily approachable from due N, by making for Les Trois Pierres lighthouse first, then leaving it a cable to the E to pass between Basse Real E-cardinal and Roche Goulin W-cardinal beacon towers. There is also an anchorage about ½ mile SSE of Les Trois Pierres, close E of the string of rocks and islands known as Les Lédénez de Molène. The safest approach is again from the N, making for Les Trois Pierres at first but then passing ½ mile E of the lighthouse and

Le Stiff, Ushant

Petit Lédénez de Molène. Fetch up in the natural bight between Grand and Petit Lédénez, about 2 cables from each. A delightful spot in gentle westerly weather. Use French SHOM Chart No 5567 and aim to arrive near slack water.

Ile de Quéménès: A small low-lying island 2 miles SE of Molène. There's an attractive anchorage in the Passe du Cromic between the E end of Quéménès and Ile de Lytiry. Approach from the SW, having reached Pierres Noires S-cardinal buoy ¾ hr before HW Brest and then made good 040°T for 5 miles to the entrance to Passe du Cromic. This track leaves La Vieille Noire E-cardinal beacon ½ mile to port. Enter Passe du Cromic from due S and fetch up about 100m NE of Quéménès slip in 1m LAT. Although this is a spot for settled weather and good visibility, there's shelter from the W once you are inside. Use French SHOM Chart No 5159.

Anse de Bertheaume: This broad bay lies just over 3 miles E of Pointe de St Mathieu and the anchorage in its SW corner is well sheltered in westerlies and north-westerlies. Fetch up outside the local moorings and be sure to avoid Le Chat, a nasty reef (dries 6.8m) lurking a cable NE of Fort de Bertheaume. You can land at the slip on the S side of the beach and a 20 minute stroll takes you to the village of Plougonvelin. Admiralty Chart No 3427 is useful.

Elorn River: This rather pleasant river flows into the Rade de Brest opposite Moulin Blanc marina. There are various anchorages in the lower reaches for 3 miles or so above Albert-Louppe bridge. Le Passage is attractive, ¾ mile above the bridge on the S side of the river; you should fetch up clear of the local moorings and buoy the anchor. A mile further upstream you can anchor off the N shore in the Anse St Nicolas, which offers better shelter than Le Passage if the wind is at all fresh from the SW. A mile above St Nicolas, there's good shelter from all quarters in the last tongue of deep water, about ¼ mile NE of St Jean red beacon tower. Use Admiralty Chart No 3427.

Anse de l'Auberlac'h: A rather crowded inlet in the Rade de Brest, entered just over a mile E of Ile Ronde and providing good

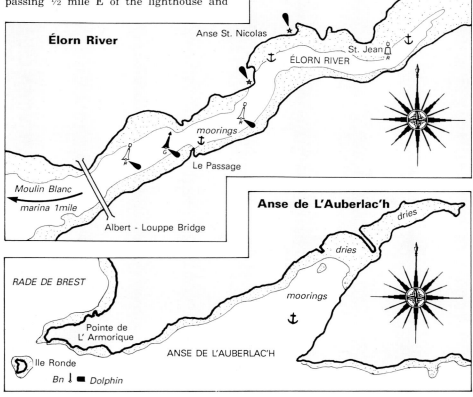

shelter in any northerly winds. You need to anchor clear of the numerous local moorings. Use Admiralty Chart No 3427.

Tinduff: A small pier harbour on the W shore of the Baie de Daoulas, which itself lies on the N side of the Aulne estuary. The Baie de Daoulas is shallow, but there's an anchorage in a pool a little way E of Tinduff pierhead, where you can lie afloat at springs with good shelter in westerlies and north-westerlies. At neaps, most yachts will be able to tuck further into the harbour and anchor clear of the local moorings, where there's good protection from between SW through W to NNE. Enter the Baie de Daoulas above half-tide, preferably on the flood, being sure to avoid the drying rock and shoals off Pointe Pen a Lan.

Rivière de Daoulas: A peaceful shallow river which flows into the E side of the Baie

Daoulas River

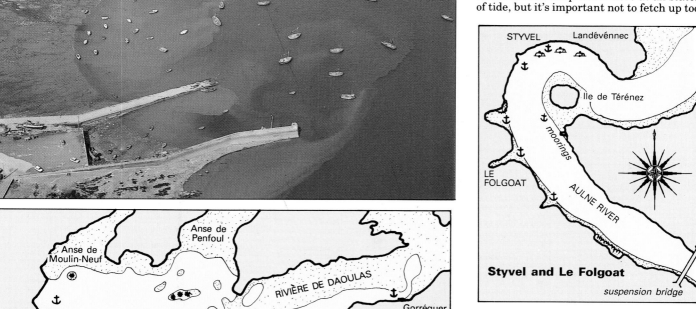

Tinduff

de Daoulas. Enter above half-tide, preferably on the flood, and anchor not quite ¾ mile above Pointe du Château close off the S side of the river near a small quay. Perfect shelter from all quarters in 1½m LAT. There's a sleepy cafe up the hill at Gorréquer and half-an-hour's walk takes you to the small town of Logonna-Daoulas. Use Admiralty Chart No 3427.

Styvel: This is the first sheltered anchorage in the Aulne river proper, just opposite Ile de Térénez and very close off the N bank. There's deep water here at all states of tide, but it's important not to fetch up too

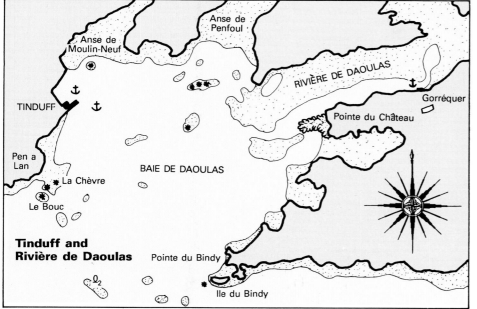

STYVEL Landévénnec
Ile de Térénez
LE FOLGOAT
moorings
AULNE RIVER

Styvel and Le Folgoat

suspension bridge

near the various large mooring buoys. Your anchor should be buoyed, in case you are unlucky enough to foul one of the ground chains.

Le Folgoat: There are various anchorages between Styvel and the suspension bridge, but the bottom is rocky away from the banks. There's good holding in mud at the mouth of either of the two drying inlets on the W side of the river, tucking in as close as the tide allows. A slight bay, just over ½ mile below the bridge on the W side, is also a good spot if you edge well inshore. On the E side of the river, you can anchor just downstream of the local moorings which are laid just above Ile de Térénez. There are several anchorages in the Aulne above

Anse de Penfoul
Anse de Moulin-Neuf
RIVIÈRE DE DAOULAS
TINDUFF
Gorréquer
Pointe du Château
Pen a Lan
La Chèvre
BAIE DE DAOULAS
Le Bouc

Tinduff and Rivière de Daoulas

Pointe du Bindy
Ile du Bindy

the suspension bridge, with landing places at Trégarvan and Le Passage.

Anse de Pen-hir: An attractive anchorage in a sandy bay just E of Pointe de Pen-Hir. Entry is straightforward from the Chenal du Toulinguet, by rounding Les Tas de Pois, a conspicuous group of five large above-water rocks which extend for ½ mile SW of Pointe de Pen-Hir. The approach from the direction of the Raz de Sein is also straightforward if you make for Les Tas de Pois first.

If coming from the S round Cap de la Chèvre, it's important to avoid Le Bouc, a low above-water rock marked on its W side by a W-cardinal buoy, and Le Chevreau (dries 6.1m) marked by a W-cardinal spar beacon. The Anse de Pen-Hir offers good shelter in winds from between W through N to E, although it can be uneasy if there's any south-westerly swell. Use Admiralty Chart No 798.

Anse de Dinan: A wide shallow bay 3 miles E of Les Tas de Pois, the Anse de Dinan offers good shelter in winds from the N and E, but is exposed to any swell from

Pt. du Raz

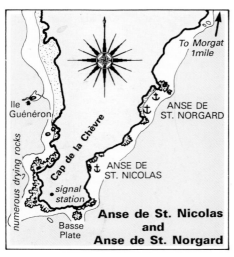

the W. Entry is straightforward from the direction of Les Tas de Pois and the best spot to anchor is usually in the NE corner of the bay.

Anse de St Nicolas: A somewhat rugged anchorage on the E side of Cap de la Chèvre, the Anse de St Nicolas is a good spot in north-westerlies. Cap de la Chèvre should be rounded a mile off and the anchorage approached from the SE. There are no dangers in the bay and you can tuck close in if the wind is offshore.

Anse de St Norgard: A small rocky bay just over a mile NNE of Anse de St Nicholas, between Pointe de Rostudel and Pointe de St Hernot. There's shelter here in westerlies and north-westerlies, although the coast is rather austere. Approach from the ESE, giving a wide berth to the drying rocks off Pointe de St Hernot.

Ile de l'Aber: An attractive anchorage 2½ miles E of Morgat entrance, close SE of Ile de l'Aber and sheltered from between NW through N to ENE. Coming from Morgat, leave Rocher de l'Aber (21m high) close to port and then turn NNE into the anchorage. Don't fetch up too close to the rocky causeway between Ile de l'Aber and the mainland.

Coming from the S, either from Douarnenez or Cap de la Chèvre, it's usually best

Douarnenez

Baie des Trépassés

cable SE of the islet of Crévendeilet, but keep clear of the fishing boat moorings and keeper-pot buoys. There's good shelter in easterlies here, although the bay is open to any westerly swell. It can be a useful spot to wait if you are early on the tide for the Raz de Sein. Approach from due W to avoid the various dangers SW of Pointe du Van. ●

to pass E of both La Pierre-Profonde (4.3m high) and Les Verrès (9m high) which lie a mile or so SSW of Ile de l'Aber. If passing W of these rocks, be sure to clear Le Taureau (dries 1.8m) which lurks not quite ¼ mile N of La Pierre-Profonde. Use Admiralty Chart No 798.

Douarnenez: There are several anchorages near Douarnenez, which can be useful if Tréboul marina or Port de Rosmeur are crowded. In quiet weather or with winds from between W through S to SE, you can anchor in the Rade du Guet, 1-2 cables ESE of Ile Tristan. At neaps, the W side of the Anse du Ris offers reasonable shelter with the wind from between W through S to E. In quiet weather or southerlies, there's a pleasant anchorage off Les Sables-Blancs, a little way W of Pouldavid river mouth.

Fetch up about 1½ cables SE of Rocher Coulinec, or a bit closer to the beach near neaps.

Baie des Trépassés: A wide shelving bay just N of the promontory which terminates in the Pointe du Raz. There's a fair-weather anchorage on the N side of the bay, about a

Baie des Trépassés

Pointe du Van

various drying rocks

✝ chapel (conspic.)

Crévendeilet

Approach from W to avoid dangers off Pointe du Van

BAIE DES TRÉPASSÉS

gradually shelving beach

Raz de Sein

La Vieille

La Plate

statue

buildings

Pointe du Raz

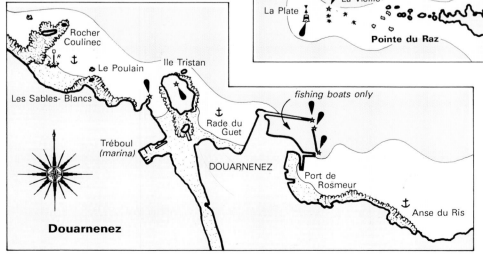

Rocher Coulinec

Le Poulain

Ile Tristan

Les Sables-Blancs

Rade du Guet

Tréboul (marina)

fishing boats only

DOUARNENEZ

Port de Rosmeur

Anse du Ris

Douarnenez

USEFUL ADMIRALTY CHARTS

No 3345 — Chenal du Four
No 3427 — Approaches to Brest
No 798 — Baie de Douarnenez

FRENCH SHOM CHARTS

No 5567 Ile d'Ouessant
No 5159 Ile de Molène

Chapter 5
Raz de Sein to Baie de la Forêt

There is a stretch of cruising 'no-man's-land' along the west coast of Brittany, which is definitely removed from the rocky Côtes du Nord but not yet within the warmer, softer waters of French Biscay. You seem to enter this transitional area at the Raz de Sein, and then hang in limbo for 20-30 miles until Pointe de Penmarc'h is safely astern and you are anchored or moored somewhere in the friendly Anse de Bénodet. In this chapter we negotiate the Raz de Sein and take a quick look at two anchorages off Ile de Sein, before lingering in no-man's-land for a while. Then, having rounded Penmarc'h and entered the Bay of Biscay proper, one can look forward to the various anchorages in the Anse de Bénodet, including the fascinating nooks and crannies around Iles de Glénan.

But first the notorious Raz de Sein, an important milestone in a passage to or from the Bay of Biscay. This uneasy and temperamental stretch of water represents both a natural and a psychological gateway between 'Channel' cruising and the warmer promise of the south. The Raz is also the subject of generations of clubroom tales which, apocryphal or not, help to maintain its somewhat sinister reputation.

The Raz de Sein is just 1½ miles wide, from the twin towers of La Plate and La Vieille across to the eastern fringe of the dangers bordering Ile de Sein. Although the tidal stream is fairly weak to the north and south of the Raz, it is powerful in the narrows. The strength and concentration of this stream, as it pours over an uneven sea bed, can result in a savage maelstrom of overfalls, especially if the tide is weather-going.

As a general rule, therefore, you should take the Raz at slack water, preferably as the stream is about to turn in your favour. Coming from the north, say from Camaret, Morgat or perhaps direct from the Chenal du Four, you would aim to be 1½ miles due east of Tevennec islet half an hour before HW Brest. Coming from the south, from Audierne or Pointe de Penmarc'h, you should be 1½ miles S by E of La Vieille light-tower at 5½ hours after HW Brest.

Slack water is equally important for the approach to Ile de Sein, so that you are not having to cope with fierce cross-tides whilst trying to pick up the leading marks. I prefer *high water* slack, because many of the isolated heads are then safely covered. There is, however, a counter argument for approaching at *low water slack*, when you can see many of the drying rocks and sound into the anchorages knowing the minimum depth of water.

Ile de Sein, covering less than half a square mile, is home to about 600 people. Devoid of trees and nowhere more than twenty feet above sea-level, the island's protection from the elements often seems distinctly tenuous. Most of the houses are on the east side, near the harbour, and they huddle only a yard or two apart in solidarity against the unrelenting wind. You soon sense that this is a highly independent community, used to a hard life and relying on its own resources for survival. The ageing population is supported by fishing, some vegetable growing, and the tourists who come by ferry from Audierne to sample a few hours of isolation before returning to mainland comforts.

The west part of the island is desolate in the extreme, a barren expanse of dunes overshadowed by the lighthouse, some power station

buildings and a rather austere chapel. You can see the swell breaking ominously over the rest of the *Chaussée de Sein*, traditionally known to English mariners as 'The Saints'. This long tail of reefs stretches west for another eight miles as far as Roche Occidentale. Five miles out is the Ar Men tower, whose construction on the outer above-water rock took the local fishermen 30 years of toil before it was completed in 1897.

Back on the mainland, the coast trends more or less due east for eight miles or so from Pointe du Raz towards Audierne. I've included two anchorages along this stretch and a third a few miles beyond Audierne at Pors-Poulhan. There is no practical scope for anchoring off the long southward sweep down to Pointe de Penmarc'h and I have eschewed any rock-dodging in the immediate vicinity of this rather bleak headland. The next feasible anchorage is in a small bay off a sandy beach just east of Lesconil harbour, a pleasant spot about five miles before the entrance to Loctudy. Loctudy itself, three miles southwest of Bénodet entrance, is accessible at almost any state of tide. This unspoilt river is well filled with moorings and now has a marina, but there is still room to anchor in the shallow upper reaches.

For many yachtsmen, the charming cruising area contained by the triangle of Loctudy, Concarneau and Iles de Glénan, seems to capture the very essence of the South Brittany coast. As you round austere Penmarc'h and follow the offshore buoys east towards the Anse de Bénodet, the whole mood of the seascape softens, the sun usually comes out, and you begin to feel properly on holiday. Beacon towers pop up all over the place, inviting you to choose from several attractive ports-of-call. The fine sandy beaches are a welcome sight after Penmarc'h and the cluster of low islands to starboard, the inimitable Iles de Glénan, holds a promise of fascinating anchorages yet to be explored.

Iles de Glénan are home to the legendary sailing school — the Centre Nautique des Glénans — which was established on Ile Cigogne shortly after the last war. This was a far-sighted project with the aim of encouraging self-reliance through seamanship in the country's up and coming generation. Glénan boats roam far and wide and I well remember the tiny but functional aluminium sloops, without engines or electronics and packed with six or more crew, which used to tack into Dartmouth after a 48 hour passage from Glénan. Perhaps it's easy to be nostalgic, but the sense of adventure associated with that kind of cruising seems difficult to recapture in our own diesel and Decca era.

Half a dozen miles east of Anse de Bénodet is a pronounced inlet known as Baie de la Forêt, with the colourful port of Concarneau in its south-east corner. At the head of the bay, a narrow dredged channel leads up a shallow creek behind Cap Coz to Port la Forêt yacht harbour. You can anchor off the entrance to this channel, just south of Cap Cos, and at Beg Meil off the south-west side of Baie de la Forêt. Opposite Beg Meil, on the Concarneau side of the bay, there are quiet spots to anchor in the Anse de Kersos, a peaceful and attractive inlet half a mile south of Concarneau harbour entrance. There are anchorages, too, as you start cruising south-east out of Baie de la Forêt and then eastwards towards the picturesque Aven and Bélon Rivers.

Raz de Sein

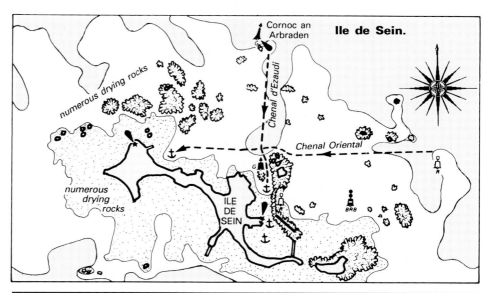

Ile de Sein: This really comes under the 'harbour' category, except that the island is so unspoilt that a visiting yacht is thrown very much onto her own resources. Ile de Sein lies just 3 miles W of the track most yachts take through the Raz de Sein, but is usually given only a fleeting glance during a passage north or south. The best time to approach is near HW Brest, when the streams are slack and you have plenty of water over many of the dangers. Use the Chenal d'Ezaudi from the N or the Chenal Oriental from the E, referring to French SHOM Chart No 5252.

The most sheltered anchorage near neaps is in the S part of the harbour, which dries at LAT. At springs you have to fetch up immediately off the lifeboat slip in order to stay afloat. The latter position is exposed to

Ile de Sein

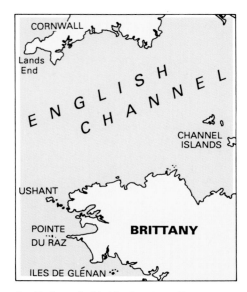

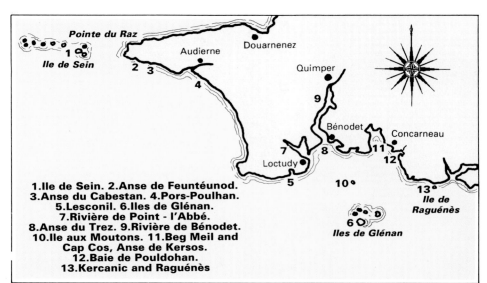

1.Ile de Sein. 2.Anse de Feuntéunod.
3.Anse du Cabestan. 4.Pors-Poulhan.
5.Lesconil. 6.Iles de Glénan.
7.Rivière de Point - l'Abbé.
8.Anse du Trez. 9.Rivière de Bénodet.
10.Ile aux Moutons. 11.Beg Meil and
Cap Cos, Anse de Kersos.
12.Baie de Pouldohan.
13.Kercanic and Raguénès

Lesconil

Aerial photographs courtesy of E. Guillemot/Blue Sky.

the E above half-tide, but is well protected from S and W.

There's another anchorage on the N side of the island in quiet weather or southerlies, which you can reach from either entrance channel once you are close N of Nerroth, Bring Ile de Sein main lighthouse bearing due W true and approach it on this line until Conolloc East red beacon tower is bearing due N true. Then edge SW towards the beach and fetch up in about 1m LAT. This bay captures the wild atmosphere of the island perfectly, but you should move round into the harbour if the wind swings out of the south or a westerly swell sets in.

Anse de Feuntéunod: A small cove on the S side of the Pointe du Raz, not quite 3 miles along the coast from La Plate beacon tower and just E of Pointe de Feuntéunod. Approach from due S at any state of tide, having rounded Pointe de Feuntéunod at least 2 cables off it coming from the Raz. There's good shelter from WNW through N to E if you edge well into the cove. If the wind shifts while you are there, Audierne is only 7 miles to the E.

Anse du Cabestan: This wide sandy bay lies 4 miles E along the coast from the Anse de Feuntéunod and only 3 miles from Audierne. It makes a pleasant anchorage in settled weather when the wind is anywhere between N and E. Approach from the SW at any state of tide, making sure that you avoid Basse du Loch (dries 2.1m) and Rocher Sud de Porz-Tarz (dries 3m) if coming along the coast from the direction of the Raz, then the St Tugen Church spire is a useful landmark behind the beach.

Pors-Poulhan: A tiny pier harbour for small local boats, 3½ miles ESE along the coast from the entrance to Audierne. You

can anchor off the entrance to Pors-Poulhan in north-easterlies and it's not far to Audierne or Ste Evette if the wind shifts.

Lesconil: This small fishing harbour lies 7 miles E of Pointe de Penmarc'h. There's rarely room to lie afloat, but you can find an

outer anchorage 3-4 cables ENE of the pierhead, sheltered from between W through N to NE. The easiest approach is from Karek Greis E-cardinal buoy, thence making good 335°T for just over 1½ miles to leave Enizan rock ¼ mile to starboard and Men Caes beacon tower 1½ cables to port. Once past Men

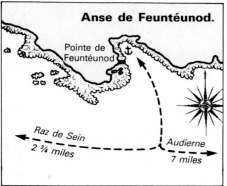

Anse de Feuntéunod.

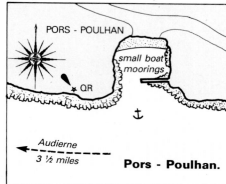

Pors - Poulhan.

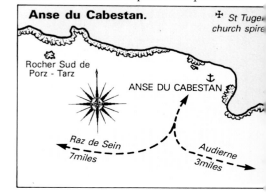

Anse du Cabestan.

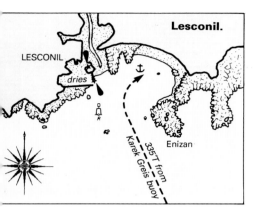

Lesconil.

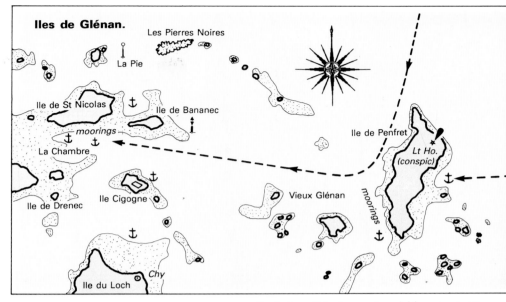

Iles de Glénan.

Caes, turn to the NE to enter the anchorage but be sure to avoid the extensive ledge of drying rocks on the E side of the bay.

Iles de Glénan: This fascinating archipelago lies 10 miles SSE of Benodet and a similar distance SSW of Concarneau. Although bordered by numerous rocks and shoals, the islands are not difficult to navigate in quiet weather with good visibility. Use Admiralty Chart No 3640 or the French SHOM Chart No 6648. The best approach for strangers is from the NNE near HW, making good about 205°T to leave the northern end of Ile de Penfret close to port. Once you are half-way along Penfret, you are effectively inside the archipelago and can follow the chart to whichever anchorage seems most protected in the prevailing conditions.

La Chambre: From the W coast of Penfret, steer a shade N of W to keep the houses on Ile St Nicolas fine on the starboard bow,

giving a good berth to the rocky shoals which extend SE from Ile Bananec. Le Chambre is the pool just S of St Nicolas and offers fair shelter from between N through W to S. Anchor clear of the moorings, but don't stay overnight unless the weather is settled.

Ile Cigogne: You can anchor off the E side of Ile Cigogne in W or SW winds. Fort Cigogne is the centre of operations for the famous Glénan Sailing School.

Ile Bananec: In moderate winds with any S in them there's a snug anchorage in the bay formed by the E side of Ile St Nicholas and

the ledge of drying rocks which extends N from Ile Bananec.

Ile du Loch: In quiet weather near neaps, you can anchor off the N side of Ile du Loch, opposite the conspicuous chimney and about 2 cables offshore.

Ile de Penfret: There's a good but often crowded anchorage off the SW side of Ile de Penfret, outside the local moorings. Penfret protects you from the E and the other islands provide shelter from the W, although you are exposed to the N. On the E side of Ile de Penfret there is an anchorage in the

Iles de Glénan

Pont L'Abbé

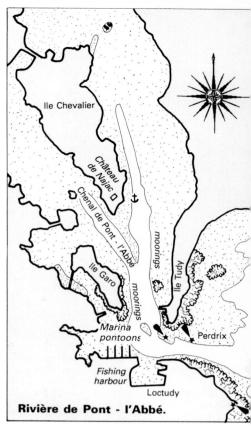

Rivière de Pont - l'Abbé.

bay just S of the lighthouse, with good shelter from the W. Approach from due E, leaving the islet on the S side of the bay a cable to port.

Rivière de Pont-l'Abbé: Loctudy and Ile Tudy are well covered by the pilot books, but there is a secluded neap anchorage a little way upstream from the main mooring area, off the SE tip of Ile Chevalier. Fetch up opposite Château de Najac, or edge further N along the island if the depth allows. Good holding in muddy sand.

Anse du Trez: This attractive sandy anchorage lies just inside the mouth of the Bénodet River on the east side. Enter the river leaving Les Verrès and Le Four green beacon towers to starboard and then turn N by E for the Anse du Trez. Anchor about 150m from the beach. There are various racing marks in the bay and you will be surrounded by small sailing dinghies during the day, but everything quietens down towards evening.

Rivière de Bénodet: Although Bénodet itself is much frequented by visiting yachts,

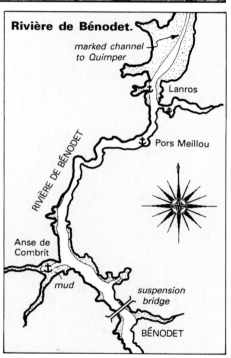

Rivière de Bénodet.

few venture far upriver above the suspension bridge. Yet there are several idyllic anchorages in the five mile stretch between the bridge and the small village of Lanros:

Anse de Combrit — On the W side of the river, just over a mile above the bridge. Keep to the N side when entering or leaving.

Pors Meillou — Three miles upstream from the Anse de Combrit on the E side of the river. Anchor well into the mouth of the inlet to find the best holding and miss the worst of the tide.

Lanros —Anchor in the bight on the W side of the river, or edge into the shallow creek just below Lanros on the E side.

Ile aux Moutons: This small uninhabited island, with its unmanned lighthouse, lies 5 miles SE of the mouth of the Bénodet River. In quiet settled weather you can anchor in the bay on the SE side of Ile aux Moutons, which offers fair shelter from winds with any north in them. Approach from the SE, having first reached a position close N of Les Pourceaux N-cardinal buoy. If coming from Bénodet or Concarneau, be

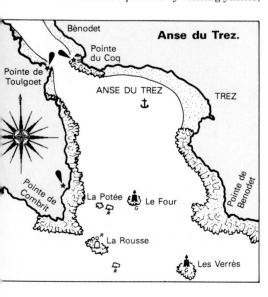

Anse du Trez.

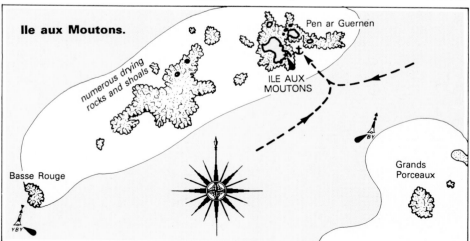

Ile aux Moutons.

Rivière de Bénodet

Ile Tudy

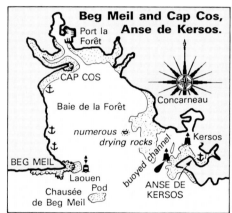

Beg Meil and Cap Cos, Anse de Kersos.

tower a good cable to starboard when entering, since there are several drying rocks between this beacon and the W shore of Anse de Kersos. The head of the inlet dries at LAT, but you can edge well in at neaps. Good

sure to clear Pen ar Guernen, a ledge of drying rocks extending E from the anchorage for about ¼ mile.

Beg Meil: Beg Meil, the low headland at the SW corner of Baie de la Forêt, is easily identified by its prominent signal station. There are various anchorages off the W shore of the bay, to the N of Beg Meil, although local moorings occupy the best spots during the summer. Avoid Laouen Jardin, some rocky patches with barely a metre over them, 3 - 4 cables N by W from Beg Meil. Also avoid a couple of rocks awash at datum, less than 2 cables N by W from Laouen Jardin. The W side of the Baie de la Forêt is not well lit, so entering or leaving at night is not straightforward.

Cap Cos: There is an anchorage in the NW corner of Baie de la Forêt, about 5-6 cables SW of Cap Cos, the low narrow spit which forms the W side of the entrance to Rivière de la Forêt. This is a sheltered spot in fresh westerlies or north-westerlies, although the holding is mixed, with some rock and gravel patches. As with Beg Meil, entering or leaving at night can be tricky.

Anse de Kersos: This peaceful and attractive inlet lies on the E side of Baie de la Forêt, ½ mile S of the entrance to Concarneau harbour. Leave Kersos green beacon

Les Moutons

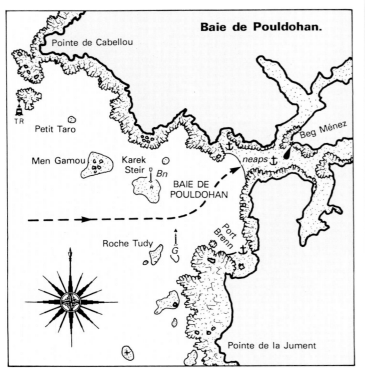

Baie de Pouldohan.

Pointe de Cabellou

TR
Petit Taro

Men Gamou

Karek Steir
Bn
R

BAIE DE POULDOHAN

Beg Ménez

neaps

Roche Tudy

G

Port Brenn

Pointe de la Jument

Pouldohan

Le Cabellou Baie de Pouldohan

Trévignon

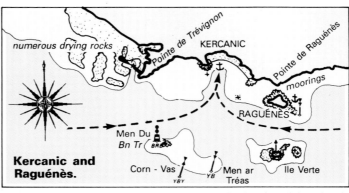

Kercanic and Raguénès.

numerous drying rocks

Pointe de Trévignon

KERCANIC

Pointe de Raguénès

moorings

RAGUÉNÈS

Men Du
Bn Tr
BR

Corn - Vas
YBY

Men ar Tréas
YB

Ile Verte

holding in mud and protected from between W through S to NE.

Baie de Pouldohan: About 1½ miles S of Concarneau, on the E side of Baie de la Forêt, the Baie de Pouldohan is bordered by a good many shoals and drying rocks. It is, however, interesting to visit in quiet or easterly weather using Admiralty Chart No 3641. Approach from a position ¾ mile S of Pointe de Cabellou and then head E to pass midway between Karek Steir red spar beacon, left to port, and Roche Tudy green beacon tower, left to starboard.

Port Brenn is a possible anchorage, in the SE corner of Baie de Pouldohan, although this narrow cove is best entered near LW so that the extent of the various reefs can easily be seen. Otherwise, sound into the river mouth as far as depth allow. It is not pru-

dent to enter at night, but it is possible to leave if necessary using Pouldohan sector light *(FlG,4s)*.

Kercanic: This wide sandy bay lies between Pointe de Trévignon and Pointe de Raguénès, but is the *second* bay E from Trévignon. In quiet weather or in winds with any N in them, you can anchor off the beach in the NW corner of Kercanic bay, just outside the moorings. The swell is uncomfortable in even light onshore winds. Coming from the W, say from Benodet or Concarneau, pass midway between Pointe de Trévignon and Men Du beacon tower; coming from the E, most yachts pass between Ile Verte and Ile Raguénès.

Raguénès: Ile de Raguénès lies close off Pointe de Raguénès, not quite 3 miles W along the coast from the mouth of the Aven

and Bélon Rivers. The E sides of the islands and headland form a shallow bay, in which a lot of small boats are moored during the season. There is an anchorage outside these moorings, accessible at all states of tide and reasonably sheltered from W through N to NE. Sound carefully as you come in, because the water is shoal for quite a long way off the beach. Fair holding in sand. ●

USEFUL ADMIRALTY CHARTS
No 2351 — Bénodet to Chaussée de Sein
No 3641 — Anse de Bénodet
No 3640 — Iles de Glénan
No 2352 — Presqu'île de Quiberon to Bénodet

USEFUL SHOM CHARTS
No 5252 — Raz de Sein
No 6648 — Iles de Glénan

Chapter 6
Aven River to Belle Ile

The anchorages in this chapter are down in that congenial area of French Biscay between the Aven River and the Quiberon peninsula, including Ile de Groix and the Atlantic side of Belle Ile. You could perhaps describe this cruising ground as 'near-Biscay' for British yachts, being accessible in a three-week cruise from most of our Channel harbours providing you aren't held up too much by weather on the way. This is a delightful coast, with sandy beaches, gentle tides and mainly straightforward pilotage.

You often experience a characteristic *vent solaire* in hot summer weather, which may set in from the west after a lunchtime calm and then blow onshore in the afternoon before veering through north-west to north by evening. The land breeze part of this cycle may start around midnight from the north-east, becoming quite brisk during the night until about breakfast time. This sun wind has to be borne in mind when choosing overnight anchorages.

The Aven and Bélon Rivers flow into a common estuary some twelve miles east round the coast from Concarneau. On the west side of this estuary, just inland from Beg-ar-Vechen lighthouse, is the village of Port Manec'h, with a good landing quay and moorings just opposite in a tongue of deep water close west of the Aven bar. There is usually room to anchor clear of the moorings.

Both the Aven and the Bélon rivers have a good many moorings, but there are still one or two places where you can lie to your own ground tackle. The Aven is interesting to explore on the last couple of hours of the flood, and with a moderate draught you can get right up to the quay at Pont Aven.

The stretch of coast between the Aven River and the approaches to Lorient tends to be missed by visiting yachts. Yet there are several small harbours and inlets which offer scope for anchoring overnight if the weather is quiet and settled. Brigneau, Merrien and Doëlan make up a fascinating trio not far east of the Aven and Bélon estuary. May or early June can be a good time to explore this area if you chance upon a friendly anticyclone; there won't be so many other yachts about and a *vent solaire* should be less likely to disturb your peace.

Three miles east of Doëlan is the rather tricky entrance to the shallow Rivière de Quimperlé. Although the bar and strong tides discourage visiting yachts, I have enjoyed some pleasant spells here when conditions were right. You certainly need either calm weather or light to moderate offshore winds, with making tides midway between neaps and springs. Timing is all important, to avoid the worst of the savage streams; you need to be entering or leaving in the hour before local high water. However, once you are safely in and anchored close under the west bank above Le Pouldu, there is no quieter spot along the South Brittany coast.

As you approach the three mile wide strait between Ile de Groix and the entrance to Lorient, the atmosphere changes yet again. The outline of Groix is mysterious from a distance, higher than you might have expected, but gradually taking shape on its north side as a welcoming,

steep-to coastline which provides a lee from any onshore swell. I have included three fair-weather anchorages along this landward facing coast, and the island's main harbour — Port Tudy — lies towards the east end. However, the two most interesting anchorages off Ile de Groix — Port St Nicolas and Loc-Maria — are on the Atlantic side, vulnerable to swell but perfectly snug during a spell of northerlies.

The approaches to Lorient are well buoyed and dredged, as befits a large commercial, fishing and naval harbour, but the big-ship channel can easily funnel yachts in and divert attention from several possible anchorages along the mainland coast opposite Ile de Groix. Keroc'h, the Anse de Stole, Larmor, Locmalo and the Anse de Goerem, are all useful natural havens off the normal cruising track, where you can enjoy a quiet and economical night. There are one or two anchorages in Lorient harbour itself, but most of the areas free from commercial or naval activity are taken up with local moorings. If you are looking for seclusion and rural surroundings, the best bet is the Blavet River, which joins the east side of the harbour just before you reach the spur leading up to the Port de Commerce yacht harbour.

From Lorient entrance, once you have cleared the outer buoys of the *Passe du Sud*, low sand dunes curve gradually south-east to the mouth of the Etel river and then south towards the Quiberon peninsula. Although the first stretch is not suitable for anchoring, I've included a few coastal niches south of Etel, off the west side of the peninsula. Any significant swell rules out these anchorages, especially overnight, but during a settled spell of easterlies, even if the winds are fresh, you can find some good shelter in the locations I have indicated.

On then to Belle Ile, whose rather forbidding profile at a distance becomes only slightly less harsh as you draw near. This is the largest of the Brittany islands, nine miles long and a good four across at its widest. The main harbour, Le Palais, lies about halfway along the landward side, with a smaller harbour, Sauzon, near the northern tip. This landward coast is the least gaunt, and there are some pleasant anchorages, reminiscent of the English West Country, in the bays south-east of Le Palais.

On the Atlantic side, the cliffs are steeper, well weathered and heavily indented, with few signs of habitation to relieve the rather intimidating façade. Some of the deeper indentations have become pronounced inlets over the centuries, and these can provide dramatic anchorages when, during a calm spell or a period of north-easterlies, the Biscay swell is temporarily at rest.

Despite its craggy aspect, pilotage around Belle Ile is fairly straightforward, with much of the coast steep-to and most of the granite visible. The tidal streams are generally moderate along the coasts, about $1\frac{1}{2}$ knots at springs, but stronger close to the north-west and south-east ends of the island — Pointe des Poulains and Pointe de Kerdonis respectively. Night navigation along the seaward coast is not recommended, although on the landward coast it's not difficult to leave any of the anchorages and make for Le Palais if necessary.

Lanriot village, Bélon River

Aven and Bélon Rivers: These picturesque rivers are well covered by the pilot books, but each year it seems more difficult to find room to anchor. You can usually fetch up off Port Manec'h, at the mouth of the Aven outside the bar, or off Port l'Hermite, a small inlet a little way into the Aven on the E side. In the Bélon River, a good spot to anchor is off the N bank about ¼ mile below Bélon quay, just downstream from the last of a line of trots.

Brigneau: This small drying harbour, 3 miles SE of the Aven River mouth, is rather susceptible to swell for taking the ground safely. In settled offshore weather, however, you can anchor and stay afloat at the entrance, a little way SSE of the outer pierhead. Approach from the SSE after half-flood, having first made a position to the E of the unit RW fairway buoy moored about ¾ mile S of the entrance. A S-cardinal buoy marks an isolated rock off the W side of the entrance and should be left 2 cables to port on the way in. A rock awash at datum, off the E side of the entrance is marked by a green spar beacon (unlit). You can enter or leave at night using the white sector of the pierhead light (Oc2,WRG,6s).

Merrien: A picturesque creek and small harbour, not quite a mile E of Brigneau. The entrance is partly protected by a drying reef which extends ½ mile seaward from the W side and whose extremity is marked by Le Cochon S-cardinal beacon. On the E side, a green spar beacon marks a patch of drying rocks 2 cables SE of Pointe de Bali. Approach from the S between Le Cochon and Pointe de Bali, bringing the white square lighthouse inside the creek in line with the

Le Bélon

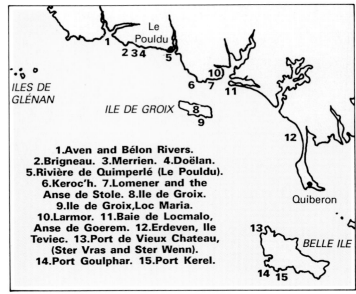

1.Aven and Bélon Rivers.
2.Brigneau. 3.Merrien. 4.Doëlan.
5.Rivière de Quimperlé (Le Pouldu).
6.Keroc'h. 7.Lomener and the
Anse de Stole. 8.Ile de Groix.
9.Ile de Groix,Loc Maria.
10.Larmor. 11.Baie de Locmalo,
Anse de Goerem. 12.Erdeven, Ile
Teviec. 13.Port de Vieux Chateau,
(Ster Vras and Ster Wenn).
14.Port Goulphar. 15.Port Kerel.

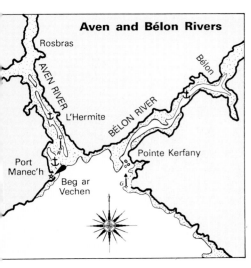

Aven and Bélon Rivers

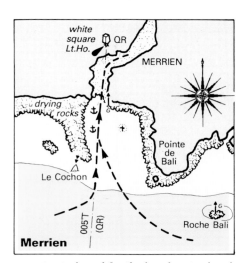

Merrien

middle of the entrance bearing 005°T. It is best to enter the outer anchorage near LW, when the rocks either side are visible. Enter the river itself above half-flood, keeping to mid-stream. The pool opposite the seaward end of the E quay dries 0.8m to soft mud, but most yachts can stay afloat here at neaps.

Doëlan: A small fishing port 2 miles E of Merrien. There is reasonable shelter inside, but the harbour is usually crowded with fishing boats and the swell can be nasty in onshore winds. In moderate offshore weather you can anchor outside, S of the pierhead. Approach Doëlan from the S, leaving Basse de la Croix beacon 1½ cables to port and Le Four beacon tower to starboard.

Rivière de Quimperlé: This rather difficult river flows into the Anse de Pouldu, 3 miles E of Doëlan. The mouth has a bar and various shifting sandbanks, and the streams in the estuary are fierce at springs. Entry

should only be attempted in offshore weather, about an hour before HW, and preferably halfway between neaps and springs. Approach the W headland of the entrance from a little W of S and make for a red beacon tower at the foot of the cliffs. Leave this tower and the red beacon beyond it about 50m to port, and then come to port until the beacon tower is in transit astern with the entrance point.

Now edge to starboard to follow the curve of the W shore into the river, leaving another red beacon to port. The channel then turns northwards, leaving a headland with a prominent hotel about 100m to port. Anchor in the pool just beyond this headland, close to the W bank and clear of the local moorings. There is a good shelter here, but do not attempt to enter or leave the estuary, in onshore winds or when there is any significant swell. Only suitable for shallow draught yachts.

Keroc'h: A small harbour on the mainland opposite Ile de Groix, ½ mile NW of Pointe du Talut. There is room to anchor clear of the local moorings and partly protected by the breakwater. Les Soeurs rocks lie to the W of the harbour and are unmarked. The safest approach is from due S, steering to leave Les Loups W-cardinal beacon tower 50m to starboard. Once past Les Loups,

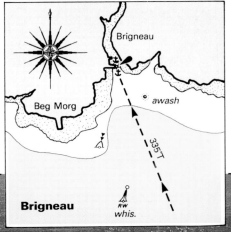

Brigneau

come to starboard for the breakwater head. Keroc'h is rather exposed from between W and NW, but is otherwise well sheltered.

Lomener and the Anse de Stole: A useful passage anchorage just over a mile E of Pointe du Talut and 1½ miles NNW of Loqueltas S-cardinal buoy, which is the outer buoy for the Passe de l'Ouest into Lorient. Approach Lomener from due S above half-tide, steering to leave Grasu S-cardinal beacon tower 2 cables to the E. Stay on a line to the E of the breakwater head to clear Les Trois Pierres (0.9m at LAT) opposite Grasu, and a smaller rocky patch (dries 0.4m) a cable S of the breakwater.

There are a lot of moorings behind the breakwater, but you can anchor just outside them to the E. Otherwise, carry on into the Anse de Stole and anchor clear of the moorings there. The Anse de Stole is bordered by wide rocky ledges, so keep near the middle of the bay - the moorings indicate the best water. Either anchorage offers good shelter in any winds with some N in them. There

L'Aven

45

are shops and hotels at Lomener, and water at the quay.

Ile de Groix, Port Tudy Roads: The attractive harbour at Port Tudy, on the N coast of Groix, is popular with visiting yachts and well covered by the pilot books. However, it is worth remembering that you can anchor to the NW of the outer breakwater in quiet weather or in moderate southerlies. This can be an agreeable option if Port Tudy is particularly over-crowded.

Ile de Groix, Beg-ar-Vir: In quiet or southerly weather there is an anchorage off the beach at Beg-ar-Vir, on the N coast of Groix about 1¼ miles W of Port Tudy and a similar distance E of Pen Men lighthouse. It is important to keep between the two ledges of drying rocks either side of the anchorage, so come in from due N, preferably near LW. Refer to French SHOM Chart No 5912.

Ile de Groix, Port St Nicolas: The SW coast of Groix is exposed to the Atlantic swell and rather inhospitable, but there is

Le Pouldu

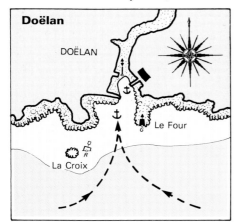
Doëlan

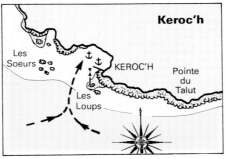
Keroc'h

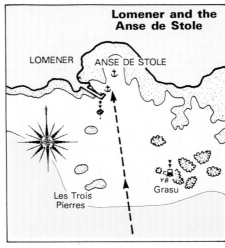
Lomener and the Anse de Stole

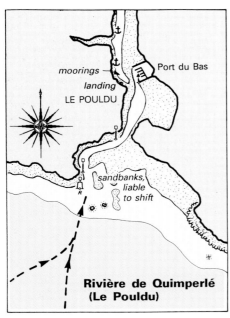
Rivière de Quimperlé (Le Pouldu)

through N to E, but clear out at the onset of any onshore wind or SWly swell. Refer to French SHOM Chart No 5912.

Ile de Groix, Loc Maria: An unspoilt natural harbour in the SE corner of Groix, ¾ mile WNW of Pointe des Chats and sheltered from winds with any N in them. Coming

Just above L'Hermite in the Aven River

an inlet between the rugged cliffs about 1¼ miles SE of Pen Men lighthouse. Make the final approach from the SW, leaving Pointe St Nicolas to starboard and heading for the middle of the inlet. Fetch up in about 2m, but watch out for a ledge of rocks which extends into the head of the cove from the N side. The bottom is sandy with plenty of rock and thick weed, so a good fisherman's anchor (buoyed) is the best bet. Port St Nicolas is sheltered from between NW

Port Tudy

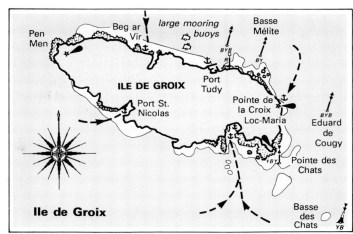
Ile de Groix

Ile de Groix, Loc Maria

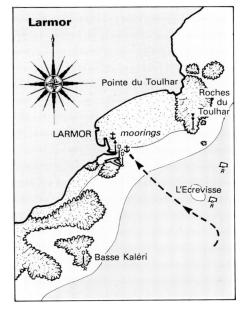
Larmor

starts filtering in. Do not attempt to enter or leave at night.

Ile de Groix, Pointe de la Croix: In quiet settled weather, you can anchor off the beach close N of Pointe de la Croix, at the NE corner of the island. This attractive spot is usually well protected from SWly swell. If you opt to stay overnight and the wind shifts, it is straightforward to move round to Port Tudy.

Larmor: A rather open anchorage on the W side of Lorient harbour entrance, but well protected from between W and N. As you are approaching the narrows at St Louis, turn to the NW at l'Ecrevisse red buoy and make for Larmor breakwater head. The final approach leaves two red spar beacons to port. Fetch up clear of the local moorings. Good shops and restaurants ashore. If the wind should shift overnight, it is easy to reach the shelter of Lorient. Use Admiralty Chart No 304.

Baie de Locmalo: This pleasant sheltered anchorage lies to the E of Lorient harbour entrance, close S of the St Louis peninsula, but you need sufficient rise of tide to enter or leave. The most straightforward approach is to turn ESE just N of La Potée de Beurre green beacon tower and then to follow the line of yellow buoys which mark the channel during the season. Leave Ile aux Souris 40m to starboard and then keep well to the N side of the narrows to pass between Petit Belorc'h red beacon tower and Grand

from the E, it is important to clear Les Chats by a safe margin, the drying rocks which extend nearly a mile S from Pointe des Chats. You don't need to go right round Basse des Chats S-cardinal buoy, but you must certainly pass within a ¼ mile of it before making any westing. The streams are quite strong at springs off this part of the island. Refer to French SHOM Chart No 5912.

From a position 1½ miles SSW of Pointe des Chats lighthouse, head N towards the beacon tower which marks the E side of the

entrance to Loc Marie bay. Leave this beacon tower to starboard and then leave a red spar beacon to port, a green beacon and then an N-cardinal beacon to starboard, and another red spar beacon to port. Anchor between this second red beacon and the pierhead, or a little further N into the bay at neaps. Clear out quickly if the forecast hints at onshore winds or if any significant swell

Port Tudy

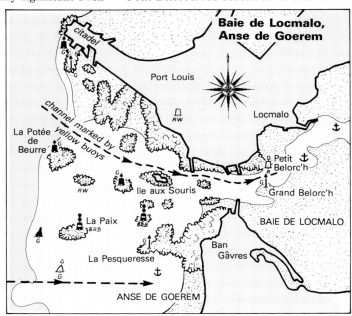
Baie de Locmalo, Anse de Goerem

Belorc'h green beacon. Anchor clear of the local moorings, but near neaps it is best to continue NE into the bay and fetch up to the ESE of Locmalo breakwater. Use Admiralty Chart No 304.

Anse de Goerem: A useful anchorage in easterlies, off the W side of the Gâvres peninsula. Make good due E from midway between Le Goeland and La Paix green buoys and fetch up about a cable S of La Pesqueresse green spar beacon, or further inshore at neaps.

Erdeven: In settled easterly weather, there are two secluded spots where you can anchor off the dunes to the SE of Pointe d'Erdeven, a couple of miles S along the coast from the Etel River. The first is opposite a narrow inlet, just ½ mile SE of Pointe d'Erdeven. It is easiest to approach near LW, when the various rocky patches surrounding the anchorage can clearly be seen. Close the coast from 1½ miles offshore, making good due E to pass midway between Poul-haut rock (3m high), left to port, and Ile Rohellan, left to starboard. Now aim to pass S of the rocky ledges bordering Pointe d'Erdeven, and N of Tréouric rock, which lies just over ¼ mile NE of Rohellan. Fetch up in 1mLAT, about 2 cables N by E of Tréouric.

The second anchorage is a mile further SE, in behind some more drying rocks which lie up to ¾ mile SE of Tréouric. Approach

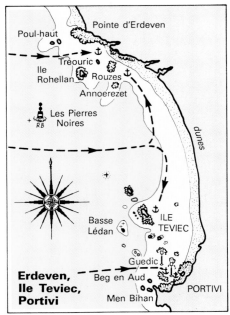

Erdeven, Ile Teviec, Portivi

from further S, leaving Les Pierres Noires beacon tower ½ mile to the N and heading E to close the beach to within ¾ mile. Now turn N along the coast, edging inside Annoerezet rock and fetching up between this rock and the shore. There is slightly less

water in this second anchorage, so it is best visited near neaps.

You need to be sure of the weather before staying overnight at either anchorage, because this stretch of coast is not safe to navigate at night. Refer to Admiralty Chart 2352 or 2353, or the French SHOM Chart 7032.

Ile Teviec: Ile Teviec lies about a mile offshore, some 4 miles S by E from Pointe d'Erdeven and 1½ miles N of Presqu'ile de Quiberon. In quiet settled weather only, there is an anchorage off its E side, with the island and the various off-lying reefs affording some protection from any slight Wly swell. Approach the coast from further N, passing ¾ mile S of Les Pierres Noires beacon tower and closing the beach to ¾ mile. Now turn S to follow the coast ¾ mile off, fetching up no closer than 2 cables E of Ile Teviec. This anchorage is not safe to leave at night.

Portivi: A small fishing harbour right on the NW corner of Presqu'ile de Quiberon. Portivi offers a pleasant anchorage in easterlies, so long as there is no significant Atlantic swell running. From a position ½ mile WNW of Ben en Aud identify Guédic red buoy and approach it from due W so as to leave the rocks off the tip of Beg en Aud a good 2 cables to the S. Come within 100m of Guédic buoy before turning to the SE and

Port Goulphar

Port Kerel

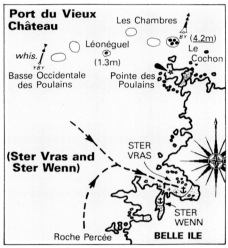
Port du Vieux Château

Les Chambres
Léonéguel
Le Cochon
(4.2m)
whis.
(1.3m)
Basse Occidentale des Poulains
Pointe des Poulains
(Ster Vras and Ster Wenn)
STER VRAS
STER WENN
Roche Percée
BELLE ILE

Port Goulphar

Goulphar Lt.Ho. (87m)
BELLE ILE
PORT GOULPHAR
Ile de Domoue
015T
010T

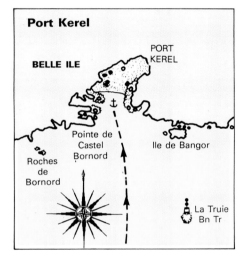
Port Kerel

PORT KEREL
BELLE ILE
Pointe de Castel Bornord
Ile de Bangor
Roches de Bornord
La Truie Bn Tr

leaving it to port. Now head towards a red beacon about 4 cables SE of Guédic, keeping midway between the two rocky ledges which enclose the channel to the harbour. At springs you should anchor before you reach this inner beacon; at neaps you can leave it close to port and edge further in towards the breakwater. It is not safe to enter or leave Portivi at night.

Belle Ile, Port du Vieux, Château (Ster Vras and Ster Wenn): This ruggedly spectacular fiord faces W between steep cliffs at the NW tip of Belle Ile, not quite a mile S of Pointe des Poulains. The approach is usually made from a position near Basse Occidentale des Poulains W-cardinal whistle buoy, but you should hold about ½ mile offshore until the mouth is well open. Keep well to the S side of Ster Vras on the way in, to avoid the various rocks off the northern point and off the N shore.

Ster Wenn is a narrow inlet in the cliffs which opens unexpectedly off the S side of Ster Vras, ¼ mile in from the southern entrance point. It offers a dramatic anchorage in wild surroundings, but can become overcrowded during summer weekends. There is barely room to swing and the local method of mooring is to fetch up in the centre of the inlet and take stern lines ashore using the dinghy. A number of rings are set into the rocks for this purpose. Although Ster Wenn

seems very sheltered once you are inside, strong onshore winds send in a dangerous surge and you must keep a close eye on the weather and the underlying swell. It is not safe to enter or leave at night. The largest scale Admiralty Chart covering Belle Ile is No 2353; it is useful for the approaches to all the island's anchorages, but you have to be careful about interpreting detail as you get close inshore.

There is an attractive anchorage off the beach at the head of Ster Vras, but you have to pick your way carefully past various rocks to reach it. Only continue beyond Ster Wenn near HW and provided there is no swell, keeping about three-quarters of the way over to the S side. Edge in slowly, with a good look-out posted forward, and leave the obvious above-water rocks to port. The various drying and submerged rocks off the cliffs to starboard are usually easy to spot in the clear water.

Belle Ile, Port Goulphar: Another craggy inlet in the cliffs, due S of Goulphar lighthouse on the S coast of Belle Ile. Although it is open to the SW and susceptible to any Atlantic swell, Goulphar is a splendid an-

chorage in quiet summer weather, especially in winds from between NW through N to NE. Stay a good ½ mile offshore until the entrance opens up and then approach from the SSW, with Goulphar lighthouse bearing between 010° and 015°T for as long as you can see it. Hold this line until you have passed between the outer rocks and then bear to starboard, keeping to the middle of the inlet. Anchor outside the local moorings.

Belle Ile, Port Kerel: This inlet faces due S and lies ¾ mile E of Pointe du Talut. The approach is straightforward, heading N true from a position about ¼ mile W of La Truie beacon tower. Anchor off the beach in the NE arm of Kerel. The sandy bottom gives fair holding, but clear out if the wind comes onshore. ●

USEFUL ADMIRALTY CHARTS
No 2352 — Quiberon to Benodet
No 304 — Lorient harbour
No 2353 — Croisic to Quiberon

USEFUL SHOM CHARTS
No 7031 —Glénan to Lorient
No 5912 — Ile de Groix
No 7032 — Lorient to Belle Ile

Chapter 7
Belle Ile to the Gulf of Morbihan

Quiberon Bay is one of those stretches of water, like Plymouth Sound or Spithead, which has that elusive aura of being steeped in history. You can somehow sense the past almost as soon as the land is hull-up — when you first spot the hard outline of Belle Ile, which partially shelters the approaches to the bay, and then pick up the low Quiberon peninsula, from which a string of rocks and shoals extends for several miles to the south-east.

Any yachtsman who has threaded the Teignouse Passage into Quiberon Bay, or the much narrower Passage du Beniguet just west of Houat island, can imagine the tensions and the fine seamanship involved when Admiral Hawke led his fleet in amongst these dangers at dusk during a winter gale, to win the famous battle against the French in 1759. No lights and whistle-buoys then, and no echo-sounders either.

Belle Ile has had a chequered past, the focus for two centuries of wrangling between England and France which began with the island's capture by the English in 1572 and ended with its being exchanged for Minorca under the Treaty of Paris in 1763. You can see the remnants of this conflict in Le Palais, where the harbour is overlooked by the rather austere citadel fortified by Vauban in the late 17th century.

It's partly all these seafaring ghosts that make you want to seek out natural anchorages hereabouts. Quiberon Bay has such a reputation for adventure under sail that it seems decadent in the extreme to lounge in large marinas at Port Haliguen, La Trinité or Crouesty. Such is the layout of the bay and its off-lying islands that you can usually find a snug retreat somewhere, and if you do get a spell of really nasty weather there are dozens of anchorages in the sheltered confines of the Morbihan.

The west side of Quiberon Bay is bounded by the Presqu'île de Quiberon and its long sandy isthmus, a popular area for the French on holiday. There are one or two anchorages off the inshore coast of the *presqu'île*, to the north of Port Haliguen. The north-west corner of Quiberon Bay has a wide shallow inlet, between the isthmus and Pointe St Colomban, before the coast curves round to the east past Carnac-Plage, La Trinité, Anse de St Philibert and the entrance to the Gulf of Morbihan. I have included several anchorages along this stretch before taking the tide through the narrow gut into the Morbihan — an intriguing expanse of landlocked water, often described as an inland sea, which has more than 50 small islands in its nine miles by five.

Sluicing in past Port Navalo and intent on avoiding Grand Mouton green beacon, your immediate choice is to bear to port for the Auray River, or come to starboard round Grand Mouton towards the main body of the gulf. The Auray River is a tempting first bet and its seven miles of wooded banks, shallow creeks and oyster beds change little over the years. The streams aren't so strong as those between the islands of the gulf, and there aren't so many other boats about. The channel is wide enough above half-tide for working up under sail, at least as far as Le Rocher, although in the lower reaches you should stay in the main fairway round the east and north of Grand Harnic islet. Just opposite Grand Harnic, to starboard, is the entrance to the peaceful Anse de Badène.

The river begins to narrow above Pointe de Kerlevarech and there are various possible anchorages up as far as Le Bono. A good spot is three quarters of a mile above Kerlevarech, off the east bank in a small bay opposite the shallow bight known as Port Espagnol. Less than a mile further upstream, the wooded banks edge close together before Le Rocher. The last stretch up to Auray is only navigable above half-tide, marked mainly by starboard-hand spar beacons. Auray is a charming old town and the St Goustan quarter, clustered around the quayside, is picturesque with many of its timbered houses dating back to the 15th century.

Back down at the Morbihan entrance, the main channel leading north-east into the gulf leaves to port the southern ends of Ile Longue, Ile Gavrinis and Ile Berder; and to starboard Er Lanic islet with its green spar beacon, and then the north end of Ile de la Jument with an off-lying green conical buoy. The tide in this stretch can be fast and turbulent, but even under sail you'll be carried through safely just by keeping to the middle.

Parts of the Morbihan are shallow, with about half the charted area shown as drying at LAT, but there are plenty of deep channels between the numerous islands and enough anchorages to keep you busy for a whole summer. Although the tide can pour through the entrance and between some of the islands at a spectacular rate, there's usually no problem about piloting your way about, once you get used to ticking off landmarks rather quickly as they flash past.

The attractive town of Vannes lies in the north-east corner of the gulf, its sheltered locked basin reached by a winding channel above Conleau narrows. Vannes is a busy provincial centre and its old quarter is enclosed by 13th century ramparts. The locked basin is a pleasant place to lie, handy for topping up with stores before you explore the anchorages of the gulf. Because Vannes is on a main line and less than three hours drive from St Malo, it makes a convenient base to leave a boat or change crews.

Outside the Gulf of Morbihan, beyond the entrance to Le Crouesty marina, the coast trends south-eastward for a couple of miles in a shallow bay between Petit Mont and Pointe du Grand Mont. I have included a couple of anchorages in this bay, which can be used overnight in north-easterlies or just for a few hours in quiet weather to wait for a fair tide into the Morbihan.

Aerial photographs by Eric Guillemot/Blue Sky

Anse St Philibert et La Trinite

Belle Ile, Port Herlin: This is more of a bay than an inlet, just over a mile E of Port Kerel and open to the S. It is a pleasant spot in quiet weather or winds from between NW through N to NE, so long as there is no Atlantic swell. Anchor about 2 cables off the beach in the middle of the bay, to avoid the various drying rocks fringing the shore.

Belle Ile, Port du Pouldon: Pointe du Pouldon lies 1½ miles ESE along the coast

from Port Herlin. So long as there is no Atlantic swell, you can anchor close N of this headland and obtain good shelter from the north-east. Approach from the WSW, leaving Pointe du Pouldon and its off-lying rocks close to starboard. Make sure that you avoid the drying rocks which extend seawards from the N side of the cove.

Belle Ile, Port Maria: An attractive anchorage off the SE coast, sheltered from be-

tween W and NW. It can be useful if you have arrived off Belle Ile from the direction of Ile d'Yeu and don't feel up to facing the rigours of Le Palais. Approach from the ESE, between Pointe de Kerezo and Pointe

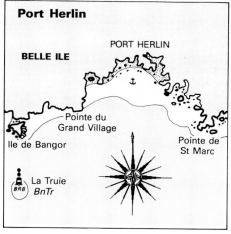

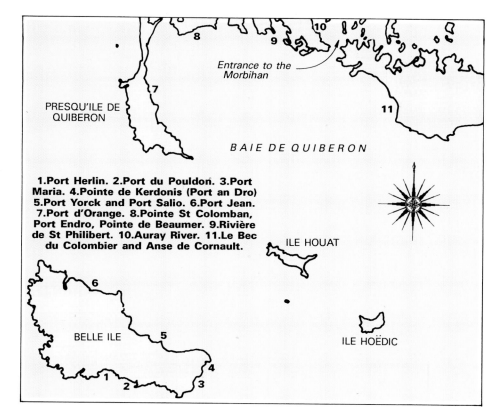

1.Port Herlin. 2.Port du Pouldon. 3.Port Maria. 4.Pointe de Kerdonis (Port an Dro) 5.Port Yorck and Port Salio. 6.Port Jean. 7.Port d'Orange. 8.Pointe St Colomban, Port Endro, Pointe de Beaumer. 9.Rivière de St Philibert. 10.Auray River. 11.Le Bec du Colombier and Anse de Cornault.

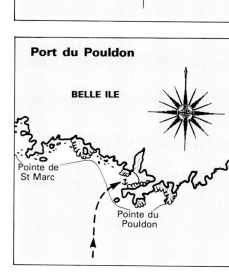

Belle Ile
Pointe du Pouldon

d'Arzic, allowing for the strongish tides off this corner of the island. Fetch up just outside the local moorings, over a sandy bottom. Port Maria has the advantage of being straightforward to leave at night if the wind should change, but it cannot be approached safely at night.

Belle Ile, Pointe de Kerdonis (Port an Dro): This is the easternmost tip of Belle Ile and there is an anchorage close S of the headland, sheltered in westerlies or northwesterlies. Approach from the SE, allowing for the strong cross-tides round this corner, and tuck well in towards the small beach

known as Port an Dro. There is good holding over sand and the anchorage is easy to leave at night. Refer to French SHOM Chart No 5911.

Belle Ile, Port Yorck: This is a useful anchorage on the NE side of Belle Ile, only 1¾ miles SE from Le Palais and sheltered from between W through S to SE. Entry is straightforward from the NE, between Le Gros Rocher and yet another La Truie beacon tower. Fetch up clear of the local moorings on the W side of the bay i.e. closer to Le Gros Rocher than to La Truie. It is easy

to leave at night and make for Le Palais if the wind should shift. Refer to French SHOM Chart No 5911.

Belle Ile, Port Salio: Just W of Port Yorck, this bay is easy to approach and is similarly protected from between W through S to SE, although it tends to be more susceptible to swell and to wash from the mainland ferries. You need to tuck close in for the quietest

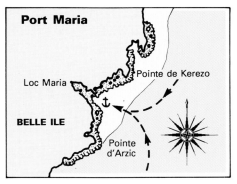

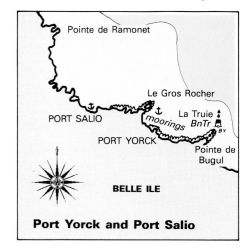

Belle Ile
Pointe de Kerdonis

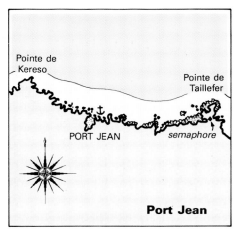

Port d'Orange

PRESQU'ILE DE QUIBERON

PORT D'ORANGE

St Pierre

Ours Kerret (dries 3m)

moorings

Ours de Kerbournec (dries 2.1m)

Beg Rohu

straightforward, finally coming in from the NNE and anchoring off a small beach. It is easy to leave at night and make for either Sauzon or Le Palais if the wind should shift.

Port d'Orange: A small drying harbour on the E side of the Quiberon Peninsula, 2¼ miles NNW of Port Haliguen. There is an anchorage off the pier, open to the E and the *vent solaire* but with excellent shelter in any winds from the W. St Pierre village has shops and several restaurants. Coming from Port Haliguen, you need to stand offshore at least ½ mile to avoid the various rocky shoals between Basse Olibarte and Les Pierre Noires. Coming from the direction of La Trinité, pass ½ mile S of Men er Roué BR spar beacon, which stands not quite 1½ miles NE of Port d'Orange. There are oyster beds in this part of Quiberon Bay, marked by yellow and orange buoys. Refer to French SHOM Chart No. 5352.

water. Le Palais is a mile to the NW and easy to reach at night if the weather changes. The best reference is the French SHOM Chart No 5911.

Belle Ile, Port Jean: A small inlet on the N coast of Belle Ile, midway between Sauzon and Pointe de Taillefer. It is only suitable in quiet weather or if the wind is from a southerly quarter, but is worth bearing in mind if Sauzon is crowded. The approach is

Pointe de Kereso

Pointe de Taillefer

PORT JEAN

semaphore

Port Jean

Carnac plage

Pointe St Colomban: A low headland in the NW corner of Quiberon Bay, on the E side of the shallow approaches to the Anse du Paux. At neaps, in quiet weather or moderate winds with any N to them, there is a shallow anchorage close W of Pointe St Colomban, with good holding in muddy sand. Refer to French SHOM Chart No 5352.

Carnac Plage (Port Endro): In quiet weather or northerlies you can anchor off Carnac Plage, about 1½-2 cables NE of Karek Pellan S-cardinal spar beacon and clear of the local moorings. Approach from due S, passing closer to Karek Bernard S-cardinal beacon than to Karek Pellan and then turning to port towards Port Endro. Sound carefully as you anchor, because the depths shoal quickly inside the two beacons. Refer to French SHOM Chart No 5352.

Pointe de Beaumer: This low promontory lies a mile E of Port Endro and its line is continued south-eastward by a narrow drying reef 3½ cables long. The reef terminates in Karek Beaumer, an above-water rock 2.1m high, which forms the E arm of a shallow bay entered by leaving Karek Beaumer to starboard and Karek Bernard S-cardinal beacon to port. There is an anchorage here in offshore winds, just outside the local moorings with good holding over muddy sand. Refer to French SHOM Chart No 5352.

Rivière de St Philibert: This shallow unspoilt river flows into Quiberon Bay a mile E of La Trinité entrance and is interesting to visit at neaps in quiet weather. Proceed as though making for La Trinité, but turn off to starboard when Ar Gazek spar beacon bears about 045°T. Steer north-east to leave this beacon a cable to port, continue past it for 2 cables on this heading, and then alter to the N towards Le Grand Pellignon spar beacon, which stands on a rock right in the mouth of the river.

Enter the estuary by leaving Le Grand Pellignon close to port and then head N by W to follow the channel, which is marked by withies. Anchor 4 cables upstream from Le Grand Pellignon, just E of Pointe de Bellec and clear of the moorings. This spot is well sheltered except in strong southerlies and has about ½ metre at LAT. The river is unlit and not safe to enter or leave at night. Refer to Admiralty Chart No 2358 or French SHOM Chart No 5352.

Auray River: This charming and inimitable 'oyster river' is well covered by the

Rivière d'Auray

Christian Fevrier/Sea and See

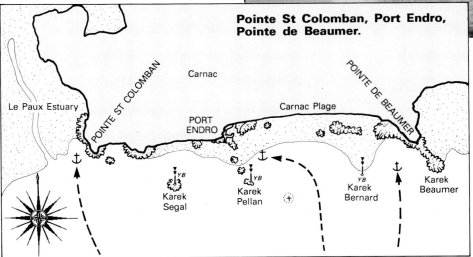

Pointe St Colomban, Port Endro, Pointe de Beaumer.

Le Paux Estuary

POINTE ST COLOMBAN

Carnac

Carnac Plage

POINTE DE BEAUMER

PORT ENDRO

Karek Segal

Karek Pellan

Karek Bernard

Karek Beaumer

pilot books, probably the best known anchorages being those in the attractive wooded narrows opposite Le Rocher. You can also fetch up in Le Bono creek, on the starboard hand just above Le Rocher, although the holding is unreliable over the rocky bottom. Further downstream, there is an anchorage on the E side of the river, in the small bay opposite Pointe d'Espagnol; you can tuck in close here at neaps, nicely out of the stream.

At neaps, boats with a modest draught can edge a little way into the Anse de Badène, turning NE out of the lower estuary opposite Grand Harnic island. The tide is strong in the gut between Pointe du Bler and Sept-Iles and it is best to enter near LW, sounding carefully. Keep well N towards the

Rivière de St Philibert

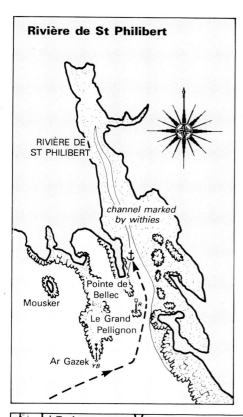

RIVIÈRE DE ST PHILIBERT

channel marked by withies

Mousker

Pointe de Bellec

Le Grand Pellignon

Ar Gazek
YB

Rivière d'Auray — plus élevé!

Auray River

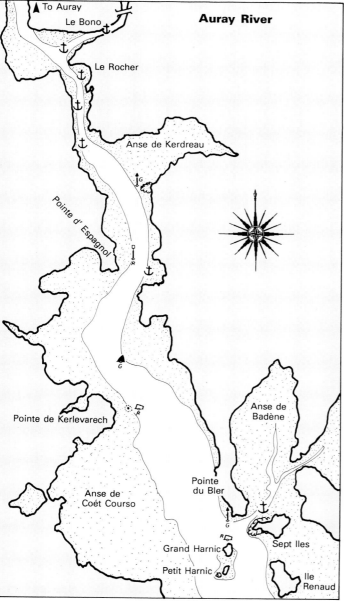

To Auray

Le Bono

Le Rocher

Anse de Kerdreau

Pointe d'Espagnol

Pointe de Kerlevarech

Anse de Coét Courso

Grand Harnic

Petit Harnic

Pointe du Bler

Anse de Badène

Sept Iles

Ile Renaud

Le Bec du Colombier and Anse de Cornault

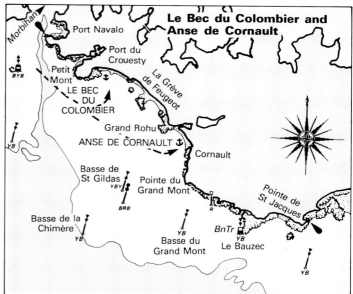

Morbihan

Port Navalo

Port du Crouesty

Petit Mont

LE BEC DU COLOMBIER

La Grève de Feugeot

Grand Rohu

ANSE DE CORNAULT

Cornault

Basse de St Gildas
YBY

Pointe du Grand Mont

Pointe de St Jacques

Basse de la Chimère
YB

Basse du Grand Mont

BnTr
YB

Le Bauzec

BRB

YB

YB

Le passage anchorage at the east end of the Morbihan

Golfe du Morbihan

outer green spar beacon and Pointe du Bler to avoid the rocky shoals off the W tip of Sept-Iles. Anse de Badène mostly dries, except for a narrow tongue extending NE from the mouth. Anchor about a cable N of Sept-Iles.

The Morbihan: There are so many delightful anchorages in the Gulf of Morbihan that it is impossible to attempt to describe them here. Neither is there any need, because the various pilot books cover a generous selection and you can easily find others with the help of Admiralty Chart No 2358 or French SHOM Chart No 3165.

One of the important considerations when choosing an anchorage in the Morbihan is to get out of the strong streams which run between many of the islands. Try to look for pronounced bays and then tuck as close inshore as you can; in most cases the bottom is muddy and there is no problem about cutting things fine and nudging aground for an hour or so around LW. If you choose a spot near local moorings, it is advisable to buoy your anchor.

Le Bec du Colombier: A little way outside the Morbihan, not quite a mile E of the entrance buoys for Crouesty marina, is the wide sandy bay of La Grève de Feugeot. The W headland of this bay, Petit Mont, is fringed with a ledge of drying rocks known as Le Bec du Colombier, but there is an anchorage 3 cables or so E of these rocks, sheltered from between N and E. The holding is good in sand and mud, but any onshore swell tends to be accentuated because the bay is shallow and gradually shelving. It is feasible to leave this anchorage at night and make for Crouesty, so long as you head S at first to obtain a safe offing from Le Bec du Colombier and Petit Mont. Refer to Admiralty Chart No 2358.

Anse de Cornault: Just over 4 miles SE of the entrance to the Morbihan is Pointe du Grand Mont, a prominent headland of steep cliffs. The Anse de Cornault, a shallow sandy bay about a mile wide, lies close N of Pointe du Grand Mont and offers a pleasant anchorage in settled weather with the wind between NE and E. As with Le Bec du Colombier, any onshore swell tends to make itself felt in the shallow water.

Although there are various shoals in the offing, the approach is not difficult from either direction along the coast: Coming from the Morbihan, make for Pointe du Grand Mont until Grand Rohu islet is abaft the port beam and then head ENE for the centre of the bay; coming from the E, say from Penerf or the Vilaine River, it's best to keep S of St Jacques and Basse du Grand Mont S-cardinal buoys before heading N for the Anse de Cornault.

Coming from seaward, make for Pointe du Grand Mont but do not confuse Basse de la Chimère and Basse du Grand Mont S-cardinal buoys — the latter must be left to the E to avoid the rock awash which it guards. Basse de St Gildas W-cardinal buoy is a useful mark, 1½ miles SW of Anse de Cornault on the seaward side of a small shoal with ½ metre over it. You can leave the anchorage at night with care and Crouesty can be reached by heading due W from Anse de Cornault until Port Navalo light (Oc3,WRG,12s) is brought onto a safe approach bearing of between 345°T and due N true. ●

USEFUL ADMIRALTY CHARTS

No 2353 — Rade de Croisic to Quiberon
No 2358 — Morbihan, inc. Rivière de Crac'h

USEFUL SHOM CHARTS

No 7032 — Lorient to Belle Ile
No 5352 — Quiberon and La Trinité

Chapter 8
Houat and Hoëdic to the Vilaine estuary

The wild twins of Houat and Hoëdic, which help protect Quiberon Bay from Biscay swell, seem to take one back in time even more than small islands usually do. Houat is the most westerly of the two, shaped on the chart like a lobster. Hoëdic is smaller, but no less independent or austere in its way of life. Houat has a good selection of anchorages to suit most winds.

The mainland between St Jacques and the Vilaine River has a few hideaways, with the upper reaches of the Penerf estuary as the most sheltered and attractive. This coast looks a shade hostile on the chart, but is actually rather attractive, with some interesting changes of mood and scenery along its length. The waters are partly sheltered by the natural breakwater provided by Houat, Hoëdic and the string of reefs stretching back to the Quiberon peninsula. In this chapter I meander as far east as Kervoyal and Billiers, both on the north side of the shallow mouth of the Vilaine.

Delightful though this whole area is, you need a certain amount of care in hazy summer conditions. Although the tides are generally moderate, some strong local sets can be experienced in unexpected directions, which may catch an over-relaxed navigator unawares.

From the Morbihan entrance, you can reckon about 10 miles to the north side of Houat and not quite 13 miles to the north side of Hoëdic.

Both these passages are simple in clear visibility and preferably with at least a couple of hours' rise of tide. But the final approach to these islands should be from more or less due north. At springs with calm winds, guard against being set to the west of either Houat or Hoëdic if, as will be likely, you are approaching on the ebb. Both islands have rocky dangers on their north-west sides.

When sailing north-eastwards from Houat or Hoëdic towards Penerf or the Vilaine, remember that, although Plateau de la Recherche has plenty of water over it most of the time, there are two isolated heads — Roche de Locmariaquer and Roche de Sarzeau — with depths of only 1.8 metres at LAT.

The entrance to Penerf is some 13 miles north-east from Houat or Hoëdic and about five miles west of the mouth of the Vilaine. There are quiet anchorages in its upper reaches and the approach is much simpler than most pilot books suggest.

The outer approaches to the Vilaine estuary are wide and shallow, with rocky dangers on the west side off Penerf. Other factors being equal, it's preferable to arrive at the entrance soon after half-flood when going in, and as near high water as possible when coming out. In fresh onshore winds, especially from the south-west, the mouth of the Vilaine should be avoided.

Houat, Tréac'h er Béniguet: Houat is a small, curiously shaped island which lies 10 miles S of the entrance to the Morbihan and about 7 miles ENE of Le Palais. Barely 2½ miles from end to end, it is part of that geological mélange of reefs and islands which straggles SE from Presqu'ile de Quiberon for nearly 15 miles as far as Les Grands Cardinaux. Although Houat has a snug harbour at the E end of its N coast, this is home to a considerable fleet of fishing boats and usually seems full even before yachts start arriving. However, the shape of the island is such that you can almost always obtain shelter off one of its splendid beaches.

Tréac'h er Béniguet is a small attractive bay right at the W tip of Houat and is a good spot in easterly weather. The approach is straightforward from the W, leaving Le Rouleau W-cardinal beacon tower to star-board and then steering for the middle of the bay to pass N of Ile Cenis and S of Ile Guric. Keep clear of the various drying rocks between Le Rouleau and Ile Cenis and those which extend SW from Ile Guric. Fetch up close off the beach in about 2m. Coming from the N through the Passage du Béniguet, pass between Le Grand Coin E-cardinal and Bonen Bras W-cardinal beacon towers and then make good about 220°T until Tréac'h er Béniguet is well open before turning E towards the bay. The anchorage is not safe to enter or leave at night since the W end of Houat is completely unlit. Admiralty Chart No 2353 is just about OK, but the French SHOM Chart No 7033 is on a slightly larger scale.

Houat, Tréac'h Salus: This bay on the S side of Houat is formed by the W shore of the sandy peninsula which extends SSE from near the village of St Gildas. Tréac'h Salus is sheltered from the NE, so it is a good spot when the vent solaire is in evidence. The approach needs care though, because many dangers lurk in the offing. High tide is best, when the streams are slack and there is plenty of depth over various rocky shoals which, although covered at LAT, can provide uneasy water for the navigator.

Coming from Le Palais or further W, it is easiest to make for Ile aux Chevaux first, but then to pass a cable NW of Le Pot de Fer isolated danger buoy. From here make good 045°T for 1½ miles, keeping the old fort on Houat fine on your port bow; this track leads between two drying rocks — Men Portz Plous ½ mile to port and Er Gadorec à Vez a little further to starboard. Edge to starboard into Tréac'h Salus as you near the coast.

Coming from the N via the Passage du Béniguet, keep a mile off the S coast of Houat until you are safely past Men Portz Plous and can turn towards the old fort on 045°T. Coming from Tréac'h er Gouret, pass close either side of Men er Houteliguet beacon tower and then skirt by ¼ mile the tail of above-water rocks forming the SE tip of the island. Once round Try Men, make good due W true until the old fort bears well E of N, to be sure of clearing Er Gadorec a Vez before turning up for Tréac'h Salus.

Tréac'h Salus is exposed to the SW and you should move round to Port de St Gildas in daylight if there is any risk of the weather picking up from that direction. Navigation anywhere in the vicinity of Houat is not safe at night. The holding in Tréac'h Salus is reasonable in moderate conditions, but the bottom is sand and rock rather than reliable mud. Admiralty Chart No 2353 is useful,

ENGLISH CHANNEL

BRITTANY

BISCAY

ILE DUMET

ILE HOUAT

ILE HOËDIC

1.Houat. 2.Hoëdic. 3.St Jacques en Sarzeau. 4.Anse de Succinio 5.Penerf and Pen - Cadenic 6.Kervoyal. 7.Port de Billiers.

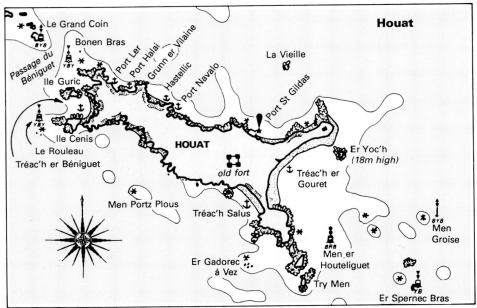

to the N. The only light on Houat is the breakwater head at Port de St Gildas (*Fl2,WG,6s*). Refer to Admiralty Chart No. 2353.

Houat, Port Navalo: One of the smaller bays towards the W end of Houat's N coast, Port Navalo lies just E of the short headland known as Er Hastellic, a mile from Port de St Gildas. The approach is straightforward, either from the N, from the W via the Passage du Béniguet, or from St Gildas itself. Navalo is snug in south-westerlies, although at night during fine summer spells it is open to the *vent solaire*. The holding is fair over a sandy bottom, and you can safely leave the anchorage at night and make for St Gildas or Crouesty. Refer to Admiralty Chart No 2353.

Houat, Hastellic: This small bay, with its attractive beach, lies just W of Port Navalo, between Grunn er Vilaine and Er Hastellic. The approach is similar to that for Navalo, except that you fetch up on the opposite side of Er Hastellic.

Houat, Port Halai and Port Ler: These two coves are next to each other at the NW tip of Houat, close E of Beg er Vachif. They are partly separated by a drying rocky spur, so make sure that you are definitely in one cove or the other. There is good shelter in southerlies, although the *vent solaire* can be a nuisance at night during fine spells. It is possible to clear out at night by heading NNE at first and then making for St Gildas or Crouesty, but you need to take careful

provided you have a good magnifying glass!

Houat, Tréac'h er Gouret: This wide sandy bay on the E coast is perhaps the most popular of the Houat anchorages and many French yachts sail out at weekends from Crouesty or the Morbihan. It is sheltered from between N through W to SW and the holding is fair if you tuck close in. The approach is easiest from the N, rounding the NE promontory of the island and then Er Yoc'h islet (23m high). Coming from the E,

say from the Vilaine River, leave Men Groise E-cardinal beacon a good 3 cables to the S before leaving Er Yoc'h to starboard and entering the bay. There are numerous dangers in the offing to the SE of Tréac'h er Gouret.

It is not safe to approach the anchorage at night, but you can leave with careful dead-reckoning by sailing out to the NE between Er Yoc'h and Men Groise beacon (unlit). Once you are clear of the island, it is easy to make for Crouesty, 9 miles away

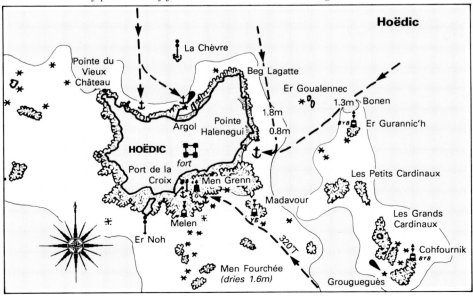

account of the tides off this corner of the island. Beware of being set W towards the dangers either side of Passage du Béniguet. Refer to Admiralty Chart No 2353.

Hoëdic, north coast: The island of Hoëdic lies just over 3 miles SE of Houat, smaller and more regular in shape than the latter, and fringed with dangers except off its N side. There are two harbours — Argol on the N coast, where the ferries land, and Port de la Croix on the S. Argol is tiny and packed with local boats, while Port de la Croix dries right out and is almost as crowded. The largest scale Admiralty Chart covering Hoëdic is No 2353.

The simplest anchorage is off the beach to the W of Argol, near the old lifeboat slip. The approach is not difficult from due N, leaving Er Rouzes E-cardinal beacon tower a mile to the W while making for the W half of the island. You can also fetch up off Argol itself, provided you keep the E pierhead bearing E of S on the approach and when you anchor. Not quite ½ mile N of this pier is La Chèvre, a patch of drying rocks marked by an isolated danger beacon. It is possible to leave either anchorage at night with care, using Argol pierhead light *(Fl,WG, 4s,11M,8M)* to keep you clear of La Chèvre and the dangers NW of Hoëdic.

Hoëdic, Pointe Halénegui: There is a secluded anchorage on the SE side of Hoëdic, just off the beach between Pointe Halénegui and Er Yoc'h bras, an above-water rock ¼ mile S of Pointe Halénegui. The easiest approach is from the N near HW, leaving the

The wild island of Hoëdic in all its glory, above. And (inset) the north coast harbour of Argol where the ferries land.

NE tip of the island, Beg Lagatte, 2 cables to the W, keeping a similar distance off the E coast and passing inside Er Goualennec islet.

If you do arrive near LW, it is important to avoid two rocky patches only just covered

at LAT, which lurk up to 2 cables E of Pointe Halénegui. Otherwise, round the headland this distance off and turn to starboard towards the anchorage, being sure to avoid the drying spur which extends SSE from Pointe Halénegui for about a cable. Do not

59

St Jacques en Sarzeau

stray S of Er Yoc'h bras, as this is only the above-water tip of a wide plateau of drying rocks stretching SSE for over 1/4 mile. Refer to Admiralty Chart No 2353.

An alternative approach is from the NE, preferably near HW, passing between Er Goualennec islet and Er Gurannic'h E-cardinal beacon tower. Bonen shoal, with 1.3m over it, lies a cable N by W of the beacon tower, but carries sufficient depth for most yachts in quiet conditions, except near LWS. Head SW for Er Yoc'h bras and turn into the anchorage as the beach starts to bear N of W.

The Halénegui anchorage is an idyllic spot if the weather is right, sheltered from between NW and W and partly protected from swell by Er Yoc'h bras plateau and the various drying rocks S of Hoëdic. It is feasible to stay overnight so long as the forecast looks OK. Leaving after dark is not advisable, although just about possible on a clear night by following the coast northwards 2 cables off. The only light is Les Grands Cardinaux *(Fl4,15s)*, 1½ miles SE of the anchorage, which can give you some-

what fine clearing lines for Er Goualennec islet and Beg Lagatte.

Hoëdic, south coast: There is a fair-weather anchorage outside Port de la Croix, with good shelter in northerlies and from the *vent solaire* overnight. The approach looks tricky on the small-scale chart, but is fairly straightforward near HW provided conditions are calm. From a position between ½ and ¾ mile due S of Les Grands Cardinaux lighthouse *(red and white, 28m high)* bring Madavour S-cardinal beacon tower in transit with the right-hand edge of Hoëdic fort bearing 320°T and follow this line shorewards. Do not confuse Madavour with Roche Melen S-cardinal beacon tower, which stands ½ mile further W.

As you draw near Madavour, leave it to starboard and curve gradually to port towards a position about ½ cable S of Menn Grenn green beacon tower. Fetch up here, take a careful sounding, and check the LW depth. At neaps you can stay afloat nearer the harbour entrance, passing between Men Grenn and a red spar beacon. Before staying overnight, you need to be sure that the wind will not shift anywhere into the S. It is not safe to leave the anchorage after dark but, *in extremis*, you could enter Port de la Croix above half-flood and try to find a vacant stretch of quay to dry out alongside.

St Jacques en Sarzeau: A small harbour at the southern tip of the Sarzeau peninsula, close E of Pointe de St Jacques and 9 miles NNE of Hoëdic. There is a neap-tide anchorage off the pierhead in quiet weather or in offshore winds from between W through N to NE. The approach needs some care to avoid Basse de St Jacques (a rocky shoal a mile SE of Pointe de St Jacques) and

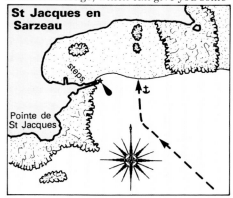

St Jacques en Sarzeau

Pointe de St Jacques
steps

Penerf and Pen - Cadenic

PEN - CADENIC

oyster beds
moorings
PENERF

withies
white tower (conspic)

Le Pignon

Borenis

Chateau de Succinio

Kervoyal

the drying ledges which lie up to ½ mile SW and S of the same promontory.

Coming from westward, say from the Morbihan, pass a good ½ mile S of Le Bauzec S-cardinal beacon tower and make for St Jacques S-cardinal buoy, 1¼ miles to the E. Leave this buoy a cable to the E before heading NNE for just over ¾ mile, keeping Pointe de St Jacques broad on the port bow. Turn for the harbour pierhead when it bears NW. Coming from the E, it can be tricky to steer a safe course between Basse de St Jacques and the various shoals off the coast; near LW it is best to approach St Jacques buoy from S of E, leave it to starboard and then head NNE.

Fetch up 100-150m ESE of the pierhead or edge further into the harbour if you can take the ground, but be sure to stay clear of the drying rocks which come well out from the E side of the bay. A riding light is advisable if you are anchoring overnight, because of local fishing boats coming and going. You can enter or leave St Jacques at night by keeping the pierhead light bearing between 290-310°T. The largest-scale Admiralty Chart is No 2353.

Anse de Succinio: This wide shallow bay lies 3 miles E along the coast from Pointe de St Jacques and makes a pleasant anchorage in quiet weather or offshore winds, so long as there is no onshore swell. There are numerous rocky shoals within and either side of the bay and it is preferable to enter near HW. From about 2 miles off, bring the ruins of Château de Succinio to bear due N mag and approach the coast slowly on this bearing, sounding carefully once you come within a mile of the beach. This track leaves an S-cardinal beacon and then Beg Lann promontory ½ mile to port.

Leave two green beacons to starboard and anchor when the inner green beacon bears due east, or edge a little further inshore if your draught and the tide allow. The anchorage is especially snug in north-westerlies, but you should clear out in good time if the wind looks like coming onshore. It is not safe to enter or leave at night. The large-

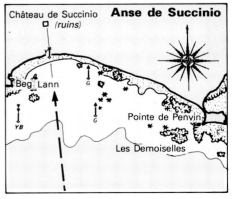

Anse de Succinio

Château de Succinio (ruins)

Beg Lann

YB

G

G

Pointe de Penvin

Les Demoiselles

Penerf

Penerf

Billiers

Men Toul

Basse
Bertrand

withies

Pointe de
Pennlan

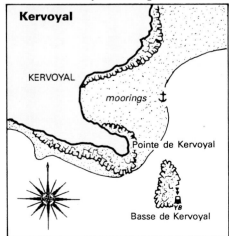

Kervoyal

KERVOYAL

moorings

Pointe de Kervoyal

Basse de Kervoyal

scale French SHOM Chart 5418 is ideal and the best Admiralty Chart is No 2353.

Penerf: This attractive unspoilt river is well covered by the pilot books, but it's worth pointing out that the shallow upper reaches opposite Pen-Cadenic usually offer better shelter than the moorings or anchorage off Penerf itself. Beyond Pen-Cadenic the river widens and becomes very shallow, although shoal draught boats can venture up the eastern arm near HW and find one or two stretches of foreshore where it is possible to take the ground.

Kervoyal: Some 4 miles E of Penerf entrance, Pointe de Kervoyal forms the W arm of the mouth of the Vilaine River. The shallow Anse de Kervoyal is tucked just behind this headland and offers a sheltered anchorage in westerlies or north-westerlies. The pilotage is straightforward as you are approaching the Vilaine from the SW — leave Basse de Kervoyal S-cardinal beacon tower about ½ mile to port and then follow round to the NW into the bay. Fetch up just outside the local moorings.

Entering Kervoyal at night is not difficult using Basse de Kervoyal (DirQ,WR). You

may leave safely by heading E and then SE until you pick up the white sector of Pennlan light. Although Admiralty Chart 2353 is adequate for the Vilaine entrance, the large-scale French SHOM Chart 2381 is much better.

Billiers: This narrow tidal harbour lies 2 miles E of Kervoyal. Although keel boats can

take the ground alongside the quay just inside the entrance, Billiers is included here mainly for the benefit of those with bilge or lifting-keelers who can continue upriver on the tide, find a perfectly sheltered anchorage and settle into soft mud as the ebb runs away. Approach 2 hrs before HW, leaving Basse Bertrand beacon tower to starboard; then follow round to the E and SE leaving Men Toul green beacon and a line of withies to starboard. The quay is to starboard as you come in, but the river turns to the N. Refer to French SHOM Chart 2381. ●

USEFUL ADMIRALTY CHARTS

No 2353 — **Rade de Croisic to Quiberon**

USEFUL SHOM CHARTS

No 5418 — **Penerf**
No 2381 — **Entrée de la Vilaine**

Chapter 9
The Vilaine River to the Loire

This final chapter looks at the last stretch of Brittany coast between two very different river estuaries — the Vilaine and the Loire. The shallow mouth of the Vilaine can be nasty in a fresh south-westerly, especially on the ebb, but you don't have to venture far upstream before tranquillity prevails and there are tempting places to drop the hook. Only two and a half miles above Tréhiguier, the Arzal barrage effectively canalises the Vilaine and there are plenty of peaceful anchorages thereafter.

The 15 miles of coast to the south of the river entrance are rarely cruised by visiting yachts, not really being on the way to anywhere in particular. However, you can find several possible anchorages between Pointe du Halguen and Le Croisic, mostly open to the west but snug in anything from the east.

Round the corner from Le Croisic, the coast is rather exposed to onshore swell, but there are one or two quiet corners near Pointe de Pen Château where you can lie overnight and escape the crowds. A few miles east of the huge marina at Le Pornichet, the Loire estuary marks the end of the Brittany coastline. The lower reaches of the Loire soon turn hostile in fresh onshore winds, belying those placid images of elegant châteaux one associates with this great river. However, I have included four possible anchorages which can be interesting when the weather is right.

The pilotage between the Vilaine and the Loire is not difficult by Brittany standards, and yet each headland that you pass on the way has its own local dangers. Off Pointe du Castelli, the first significant headland south of the Vilaine entrance, the rocks and shoals of Plateau de Piriac spread out for a good one and a half miles to the north and north-east. To the west, the ledges known as Les Bayonelles extend about three quarters of a mile off Castelli, marked at their limit by a west-cardinal buoy.

The tiny island of Ile Dumet, a recognized bird sanctuary, lies three miles north-west of Pointe du Castelli. I have included a fair-weather anchorage off Dumet's east coast, but there are some dangers to bear in mind if you are just sailing past for a look see. The Plateau de l'Ile Dumet is quite a large area of rocky shoals extending north and east from the island for up to one and a half miles. The shallowest heads, about half a mile east-north-east of the lighthouse, have less than a

metre over them at LAT. There are also various drying rocks up to four cables east by south of the lighthouse point.

Pointe du Castelli forms the northern arm of the five-mile sweep of Rade de Croisic. The southern headland of this bay, Pointe du Croisic, has some rocky dangers off its north and north-west sides which are cleared, if you are simply rounding the point from the north or south, by passing outside Basse Castouillet west-cardinal buoy.

About three and a half miles west of Pointe du Croisic lurks the potentially dangerous Plateau du Four, marked by a lighthouse at its north end and by a north and a south-cardinal buoy. Le Four is no problem in reasonable visibility, but give it an extra wide berth if conditions are at all murky.

The six straight miles of coast between Pointe du Croisic and Pointe de Pen Château are mostly steep-to, except for a couple of rocky heads over Basse Lovre about half-way along. These patches, with less than a metre over them, extend half a mile offshore and are marked, rather perversely, by a west-cardinal buoy. La Blanche rocks lie well offshore, five miles to the south of Basse Lovre, but pose no threat if you are coasting close in.

Finally, a long tail of rocks straggles out for three miles south-east of Pointe de Pen Château, partly sheltering the shallow bay now somewhat dominated by Pornichet marina. Entering this bay from the west, you pass through a narrow gateway of two lateral buoys just off Pen Château, after which the pilotage is straightforward.

The wide estuary of the Loire, like that of all the grand French rivers, is well littered with drying sandbanks in a kind of delta formation. The main shipping channel — La Passe des Charpentiers — is well buoyed, leading close in towards the west shore of the estuary from the south-south-west and more or less following this side of the river as far as St Nazaire. Yachts are well advised to follow this channel, perhaps keeping just the wrong side of the buoys if traffic is heavy. The channel has plenty of water at any state of tide, but the streams are strong and you need to carry them in your favour. It's best to enter the estuary on the second half of the flood and leave soon after high water. The Loire should be avoided in fresh south-westerlies, when the approaches are decidedly rough-going.

Barrage d'Arzal on La Vilaine

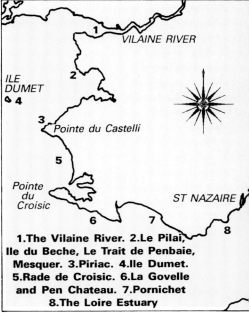

VILAINE RIVER

ILE DUMET

Pointe du Castelli

Pointe du Croisic

ST NAZAIRE

1.The Vilaine River. 2.Le Pilai, Ile du Beche, Le Trait de Penbaie, Mesquer. 3.Piriac. 4.Ile Dumet. 5.Rade de Croisic. 6.La Govelle and Pen Chateau. 7.Pornichet 8.The Loire Estuary

La Vilaine — Tréhiguier: Entering the Vilaine is straightforward in moderate weather, but the mouth is shallow and can be rough in strong winds from between W and S, especially on the ebb. Wide sand-flats extend from either shore for the first couple of miles above Pennlan and Pointe du Halguen, so it's important to follow the buoyed channel. The river narrows as you reach Pointe du Scal and then Tréhiguier village appears on the south bank.

Tréhiguier is an attractive spot and a useful anchorage, close enough to the mouth to be handy for passage-making and far enough upstream to be fairly sheltered in

most conditions. You get an uncomfortable chop in strong westerlies when the tide is running out, but the holding is good in soft mud. Fetch up well clear of the moorings and buoy the anchor. You can land at the slip and there are a few shops and a restaurant ashore. Admiralty Chart 2353 is adequate and the large-scale French SHOM Chart 2381 covers the Vilaine entrance in detail as far as Tréhiguier.

La Vilaine — La Grée: In westerlies you can find better shelter about a mile further upstream off the S bank, opposite a low stretch of marshy shore near the hamlet of

La Grée-Kerdréan. If you tuck in as close as your draught allows, the southward curve of the river gives protection from the W. The holding is good in soft mud. This peaceful spot is more secluded than Tréhiguier, but the small town of Camoël is only two kilometres inland.

La Vilaine — Le Magues: There is an anchorage off the N shore of the Vilaine, not far below the Arzal barrage at the mouth of a shallow inlet in the crook of the river bend. This is a useful spot if you have come upstream in the late evening and missed the last lock through the barrage.

La Vilaine - La Vieille Roche: This once secluded anchorage, just below the barrage off the S bank, is now packed with moorings. There is still some room to fetch up outside the trots, or you can sometimes find a vacant buoy. La Vieille Roche is perfectly sheltered in strong south-westerlies and very handy for the lock.

La Vilaine — Above Arzal: There is no room to anchor for the first mile above the

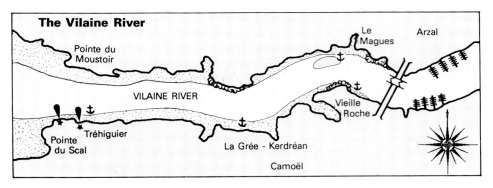

The Vilaine River

Pointe du Moustoir

VILAINE RIVER

Le Magues

Arzal

Vieille Roche

Pointe du Scal

Tréhiguier

La Grée - Kerdréan

Camoël

Plateau de L'Ile Dumet

ILE
DUMET

Ile Dumet

*Ile Dumet
(you're not supposed
to land without the
warden's permission)*

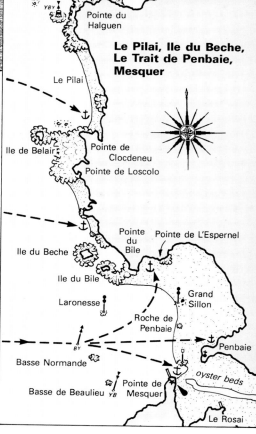

Pointe du
Halguen

**Le Pilai, Ile du Beche,
Le Trait de Penbaie,
Mesquer**

Le Pilai

Ile de Belair

Pointe de
Clocdeneu

Pointe de Loscolo

Pointe
du
Bile

Pointe de L'Espernel

Ile du Beche

Ile du Bile

Grand
Sillon

Laronesse

Roche de
Penbaie

Penbaie

Basse Normande

oyster beds

Basse de Beaulieu

Pointe de
Mesquer

Le Rosai

Arzal barrage, where both sides of the river are almost completely given over to marina berths, boatyards and moorings. Thereafter, there are plenty of possible anchorages in what is effectively a tideless lake — you simply choose a likely spot and edge towards the bank with an eye on the echo-sounder.

The pontoon berths at La Roche Bernard are very peaceful, whether you opt for the Port Neuf, just below the suspension bridge, or the rather sleepy Vieux Port in the inlet a little further downstream. There are various anchorages in the river beyond La Roche Bernard, of which Foleux is one of the most picturesque, about 1¾ miles above the bridge off the N bank.

Le Pilai: From Pointe du Halguen, which is the east headland of the mouth of the Vilaine River, the coast trends southward in a series of shallow bays. About 1½ miles S of Pointe du Halguen is a small bay called Le Pilai, just N of Pointe de Clocdeneu and Ile de Belair. There is an anchorage here in quiet or easterly weather, with Ile de Belair bearing SSW ½ mile distant, or a little closer inshore if your draught and the tide allow.

The approach is straightforward, so long as you give a wide berth to Pointe de Loscolo and its off-lying rocky shoals if coming from

the S. Don't cut inside Ile de Belair because there are drying rocks in the whole area between Pointe de Clocdeneu, Pointe de Loscolo and the island. Although it's not safe to enter the anchorage at night, you can leave by heading WNW until you pick up the sectors of Pennlan light. If the wind should shift onshore and you are forced to clear out, the Vilaine is not far away. Admiralty Chart 2353 is adequate for Le Pilai, but the large-scale French SHOM Chart 2381 is preferable.

Ile du Béche: About 1½ miles S along the coast from Ile de Belair there are two more small islands — Ile du Béche and Ile du Bile. Both are fringed with drying rocks and there are extensive rocky ledges between the islands and the shore. In quiet or easterly weather, and provided there is no swell, you can anchor off a small beach, ¼ mile due N of Ile du Béche.

This is a little used anchorage, well away from the madding crowd. Having identified the two islands, approach the beach from a little N of W, making sure you avoid the drying rock which lurks 2 cables W by N of Ile du Béche. Near LW watch out for Basse du Bile, with a least depth of ½ metre, not quite a mile W of Ile du Béche. You can leave this anchorage at night by heading WNW until you pick up the sectors of Pennlan light. The mouth of the Vilaine is only 4 miles away. Admiralty Chart 2353 is the largest scale available.

Le Trait de Penbaie: This shallow inlet is about a mile square and lies between Pointe du Bile and Pointe de Penbaie, just round the corner from Ile du Béche. Although Trait de Penbaie mostly dries at LAT, there are two neap-tide anchorages where boats of modest draught can stay afloat, one sheltered from northerlies and the other from easterlies. Coming into the bay, you need to avoid the extensive rocky ledges off Pointe du Bile, an isolated drying rock (marked by Laronesse spar beacon) 3 cables SW of these ledges, and two drying rocks in the middle of the entrance — Grand Sillon (marked by a spar beacon) and Roche de Penbaie.

Approach from due W, leaving Basse Normande N-cardinal buoy close to starboard, and then head ENE for Grand Sillon beacon, leaving Laronesse beacon ¼ mile to port. When Pointe du Bile bears due N true, you have a choice of turning left or right.

For shelter from the N, come to port towards Pointe de l'Espernel, keeping Le Leste church spire fine on your port bow but finally turning NNW to fetch up in the bay between Pointe du Bile and Pointe de l'Espernel. For shelter from the E or SE, make for the small cove which lies about 4 cables SE of Grand Sillon beacon, avoiding the drying rocks either side of the mouth.

Le Trait de Penbaie is an interesting natural haven to visit provided the weather is fair and settled, but you need to clear out if the wind should shift to the W or SW. Although it is not safe for strangers to enter at night, you can escape if necessary by using careful clearing bearings on Pointe de Mesquer light. Refer to Admiralty Chart No 2353 or French SHOM Chart No 7033.

Port de Mesquer: This small drying harbour lies close E of Pointe de Mesquer, less than ½ mile SW of Pointe de Penbaie, and is partly protected from the W by a jetty which extends N from Pointe de Mesquer. On the approach, leave Basse Normande buoy close to the S and then steer ESE towards the jetty head. Round the jetty a cable off, entering the harbour between it and a red spar beacon. At neaps, in quiet or easterly weather, yachts with a moderate draught can anchor E of the jetty, outside the local moorings. If you can take the ground easily, there is better shelter further into the harbour, but keep clear of the oyster beds in the area between Pointe de Penbaie and Le Rosai quay.

Mesquer is a restful spot, nicely off the beaten track, and there are shops in the village 2 kilometres inland. The anchorage is fairly snug in a strong south-westerly, but exposed to winds from between WSW through W to N. Strangers should not approach in fresh onshore weather or at night, but you can leave at night by using the sectors of Mesquer light. Basse Normande buoy is unlit. Refer to Admiralty Chart 2353 or the French SHOM Chart 7033.

Piriac: A small drying harbour, 4 miles SW along the coast from Pointe de Mesquer and not quite a mile NE of Pointe du Castelli. The harbour is only tenable if you can take the ground, but there is a neap-tide anchorage outside in quiet weather or perhaps a settled southerly or south-easterly. There are numerous off-lying rocks and shoals NW of Piriac and around Pointe du Castelli, so

Piriac

you have to approach from a little E of N, preferably within 2 hrs of HW. Because of this angle of approach, it is usually easiest to call at Piriac when en route from the Vilaine.

From a position 3½ miles due E of Ile Dumet lighthouse, make good 195°T towards Piriac breakwater head. As you draw inshore, look out for Le Grand Norven N-cardinal spar beacon — to be left ¼ mile to starboard — and then the red and green spar beacons which mark the channel to the outer anchorage. Le Grand Norven is often rather difficult to see and should not be confused with Les Rohtres N-cardinal beacon tower some 3 cables further to the SW.

Fetch up as near as possible to the outer moorings, whose positions indicate where the bottom is sand rather than rock. As well as buoying the anchor you need to keep an eye on your swinging circle, because there are various rocky ledges quite close to the mooring area. It is not wise for strangers to enter the anchorage at night, but you can leave safely in the white sector of the breakwater light. If you venture into Piriac harbour on the tide, watch out for the boulder breakwater on the E side of the entrance — it pratically covers near HW and is marked by a red spar beacon. The French SHOM Chart No 7033 is the most useful.

Ile Dumet: This low, rather barren island is only ⅓ mile long and lies 7 miles SW of the mouth of the Vilaine. Its sole inhabitant is the warden who protects the interests of the bird sanctuary established there. Ile Dumet is fringed by various drying rocks and by the shallow Plateau d'Ile Dumet, but you can approach from the NE and anchor off the E shore in quiet settled weather.

Before you are 2 miles off, bring Ile Dumet lighthouse (near the E tip) to bear 215°T and approach on this line. Don't let the lighthouse bear more than 215°, or you will come too close to the shallowest parts of the Plateau. The shore on this side of the island is fairly clean and you can fetch up about a cable off, with the lighthouse bearing SW. This anchorage is easy to leave at night. Use Admiralty Chart 2353 or French SHOM Chart 7033.

Rade de Croisic: This broad bight is 4½ miles across and faces W between Pointe du Castelli and Pointe du Croisic. At the head

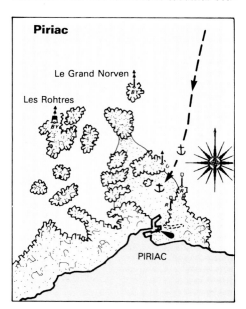

Piriac

Le Grand Norven

Les Rohtres

PIRIAC

Le Croisic

of the Rade, between the two harbours of La Turballe and Le Croisic, there is a long beach which is clear of dangers and towards which the depth shelves gradually. You can anchor off this beach in any winds from the E, provided there is no onshore swell.

The approach is straightforward from more or less due W, so long as you avoid the various rocky shoals off Pointe du Castelli or Pointe du Croisic by passing outside Les

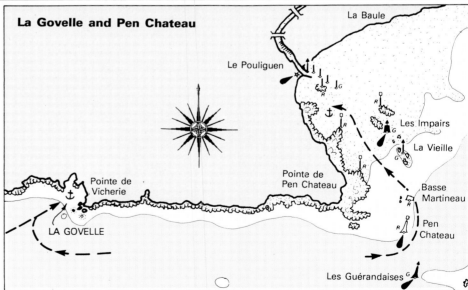

La Govelle and Pen Chateau

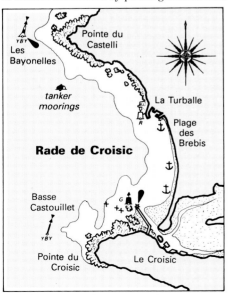

Rade de Croisic

Bayonelles or Basse Castouillet W-cardinal buoys respectively. A convenient spot to fetch up is about ¼ mile SE of the entrance to La Turballe harbour, off the Plage des Brebis. You can easily reach or leave this anchorage at night, using the white sector of the main breakwater light, but be sure to give a wide berth to the drying rocks which extend S from the E breakwater for nearly 200m. Refer to Admiralty Chart 2353 or the

French SHOM Charts 7033 and 6826.

La Govelle: Rounding Pointe du Croisic for the Chenal du Nord, you come across a 6 mile stretch of low indented cliffs and small rocky coves. At its E end this attractive coastline terminates in Pointe de Pen Château, around and to the N of which lies the entrance to Le Pouliguen. But 1½ miles WNW of Pen Château there is a narrow inlet known as La Govelle, where you can anchor in winds from between N and NE, provided there is no onshore swell.

The final approach is from the WSW, making a slight angle to the coast to avoid two isolated rocks off Pointe de Vicherie, on the E side of the inlet. Coming from Pointe du Croisic, pass S of Basse Lovre buoy, from which La Govelle lies 1½ miles to the E. Coming from Pen Château, give Pointe de Vicherie an offing of 3 cables before turning into La Govelle. The anchorage is safe to leave at night by heading WSW until you are clear of the coast and Basse Lovre. Refer to the French SHOM Charts 6825 and 6826.

Pen Château: If you can take the ground easily, there is a drying anchorage ½ mile N of Pointe de Pen Château, just W of the narrow entrance channel which leads into Le Pouliguen. This spot is preferable to the crowded harbour during high season and is well protected from winds with any west in them. The pilot books cover Le Pouliguen, which is tucked into the NW corner of a wide bay cordoned by a string of drying reefs. You need to enter near HW.

The simplest approach is from the W, passing between Pen Château red buoy and Les Guérandaises green conical. Head N by E to leave Basse Martineau red can to port before turning NW to leave La Vieille green spar beacon and Les Impairs green beacon tower to starboard, and two red spar beacons to port. The anchorage lies to port after the second red beacon. Entering or leaving at night is not advisable, but Le Pouliguen is close if the wind should shift. The most useful chart is Admiralty 3216.

Pornichet: The huge yacht harbour at Pornichet is a veritable nautical parking lot, with every conceivable facility and a high tariff to match. In quiet weather near neaps, however, you can anchor in the bay about ½ mile N by W of the harbour entrance. Approach from Pen Château buoy as though you were bound for the marina, but steer for the beach so as to pass well N of the outer breakwater head. Keep an eye on the echosounder as you come in, because the bay is very shallow close inshore. Fetch up opposite the large hotel towards the W end of Pornichet sea front.

The off-lying reefs keep out much of the swell which would otherwise be sent in by a sea breeze, although there is usually a persistent roll in this gradually shelving bay unless the weather is definitely offshore. If you anchor overnight, it is easy to slip into

Pen Château

Pornichet

Le Croisic

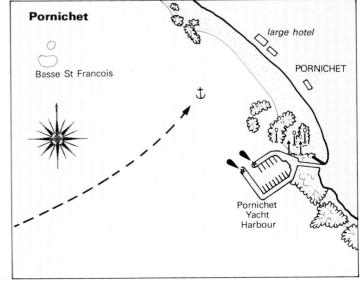

Pornichet

Basse St Francois

large hotel

PORNICHET

Pornichet Yacht Harbour

Le parking lot at Pornichet

the marina if the wind should shift. Refer to Admiralty Charts 3216 and 2989, or the French SHOM Charts 6825 and 6797.

The Loire Estuary: As you round Pointe de Chemoulin to enter the Loire, the Brittany coast is almost at an end. The Loire is one of the great rivers of France and its estuary, like that of the Seine and the Gironde, can be rather bleak. The shipping fairway is deep and well-buoyed, but there are extensive flats of drying sand across most of the mouth. The main entrance channel, the Passe des Charpentiers, hugs the W shore up to St Nazaire, and there are one or two possible anchorages in these lower reaches.

The Loire Estuary — Anse de Trébezy:

This small bay lies on the W side of the estuary, just opposite Trébezy red buoy and not quite ½ mile above Aiguillon light. The simplest approach is to edge close inshore off Aiguillon and then follow the line of the bank to the anchorage. Watch out for Roche Trébezy (awash at LAT) which lies close N of Trébezy buoy, and don't cut too close to the point on the S side of Anse de Trébezy.

There is a spar beacon just outside the drying line at the mouth of the bay, which is useful when you are deciding where to anchor. Tuck in as close as you can, to avoid the worst of the tide, and set a riding light if you are staying overnight. The anchorage is snug in westerlies or north-westerlies and is easy to leave at night, either to make for the open sea or to venture further up the

Loire. The best reference is Admiralty Chart 2989.

The Loire Estuary — Bonne Anse: There is a useful anchorage ¾ mile upstream from Trébezy, in the bight between La Rougeole islet and Villez-Martin jetty. A good spot out of the tide is about 1½ cables E by N of La Rougeole, but avoid the drying rock which lies within a cable NE of the islet. Bonne Anse is protected from between N and W and is easy to enter or leave at night in reasonable visibility. Refer to Admiralty Chart 2989.

The Loire Estuary — Villez-Martin: A small harbour on the W shore of the estuary, opposite Les Morées light-tower and just over a mile below St Nazaire. You can anchor about 1½ cables E by S of Villez-Martin pierhead, clear of the local moorings. This spot is rather more exposed than the previous two anchorages and only offers any real shelter in north-westerlies. Be careful to avoid the drying ledges which extend well out from the pierhead and from the point to the N of the anchorage. It is important to set a riding light if you are staying overnight. Villez-Martin is easy to leave at night and is close to St Nazaire. Refer to Admiralty Chart No 2989. ●

USEFUL ADMIRALTY CHARTS

No 2353 — Rade de Croisic to Quiberon
No 3216 — Approaches to La Loire
No 2989 — Entrance to La Loire

USEFUL SHOM CHARTS

Nos 2381, 5418, 6797, 6825, 6826, 7033.

French charts are obtainable by post from: Kelvin Hughes Ltd, 145 Minories, London, EC3N 1NH. Tel: 071 709 9076.

The Loire Estuary

St Nazaire
Villez - Martin
Anse de Portcé
Anse de Trébezy
La Rougeole
Bonne Anse
GRANDE RADE
Aiguillon
Roche Trébezy
Pointe de Lèvre
BANC DES MORÉES
Tour des Morées

Tidal Streams
The English Channel and Western Approaches

Based on High Water Cherbourg

The chartlets reproduced here are by the kind permission of SHOM (Le Service Hydrographique et Océanographique de la Marine — Paris) and are taken from Atlas de Courants de Marée No 551.

The stream rate for springs and neaps is shown adjacent to the directional arrows. A more precise rate can be obtained by the use of the tidal-coefficient system which is published by SHOM and available from BP 426 - 29275 Brest Cedex France.

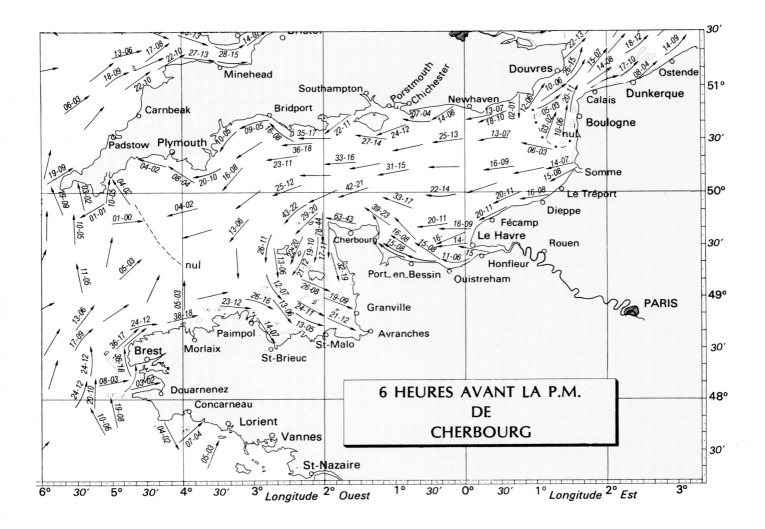

6 HEURES AVANT LA P.M.
DE
CHERBOURG

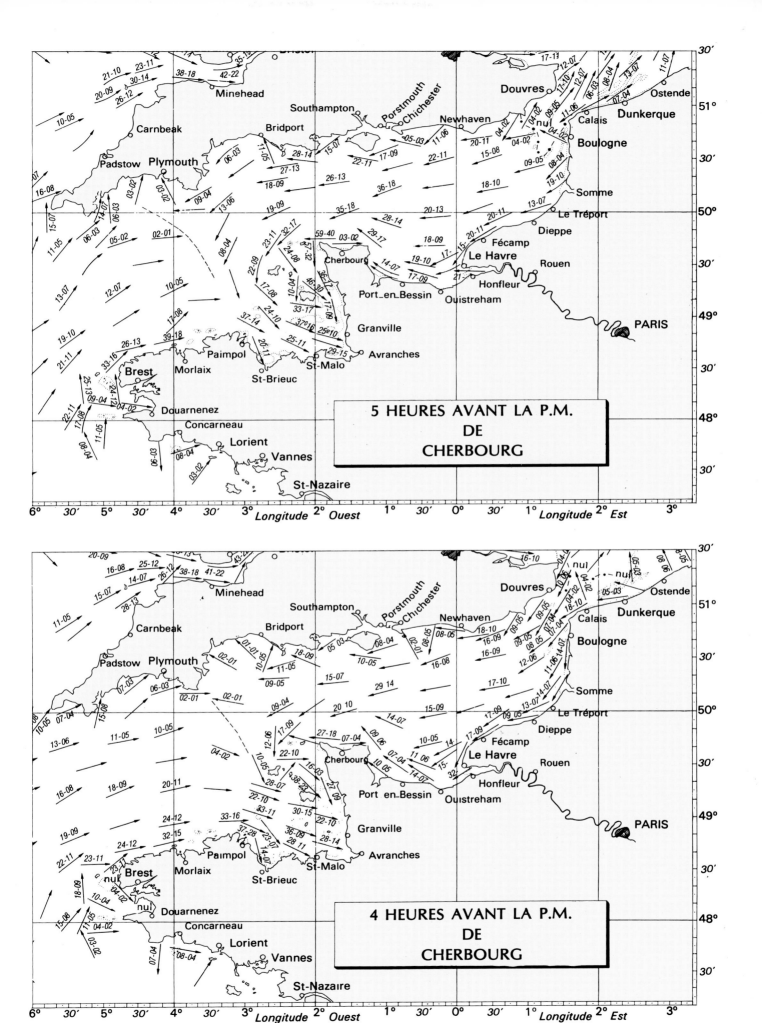

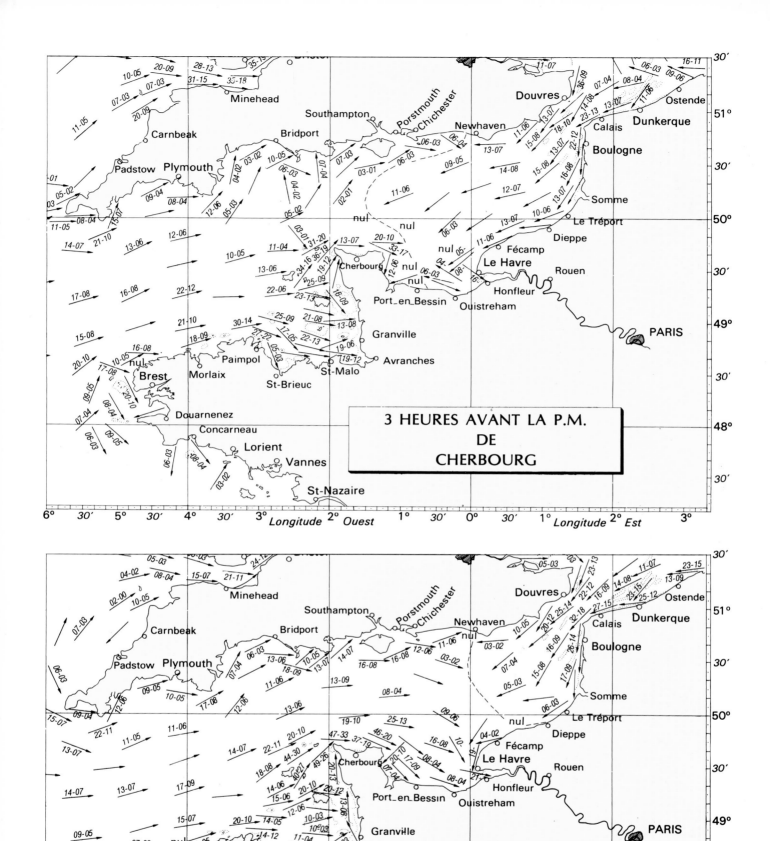

3 HEURES AVANT LA P.M. DE CHERBOURG

2 HEURES AVANT LA P.M. DE CHERBOURG

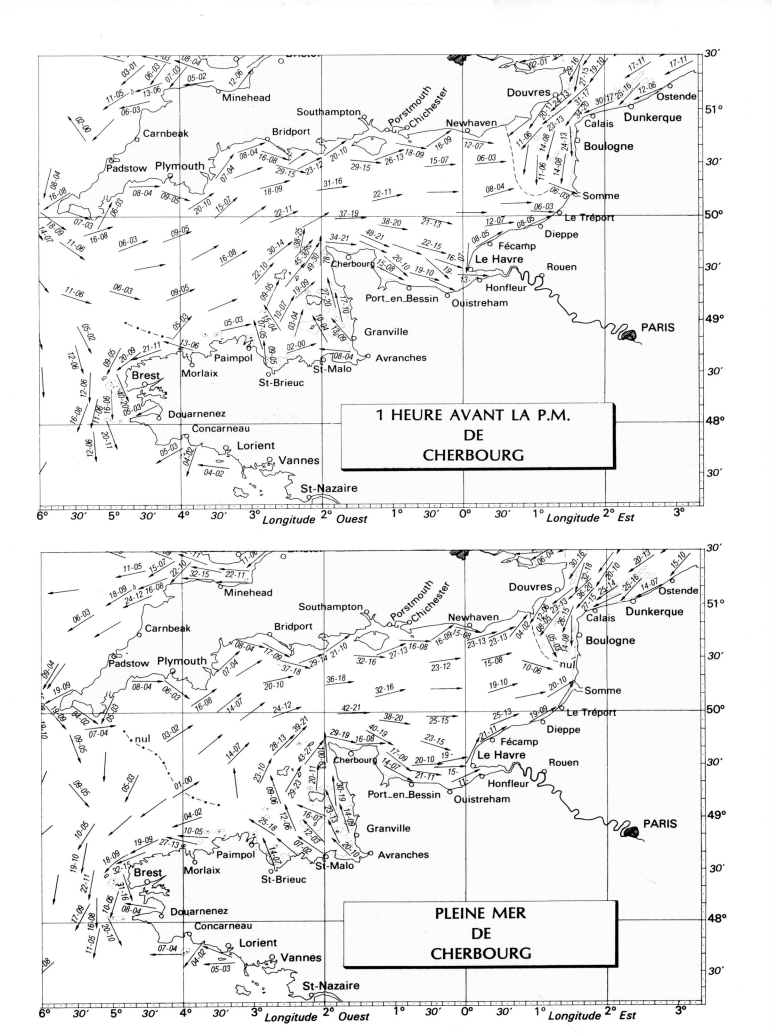

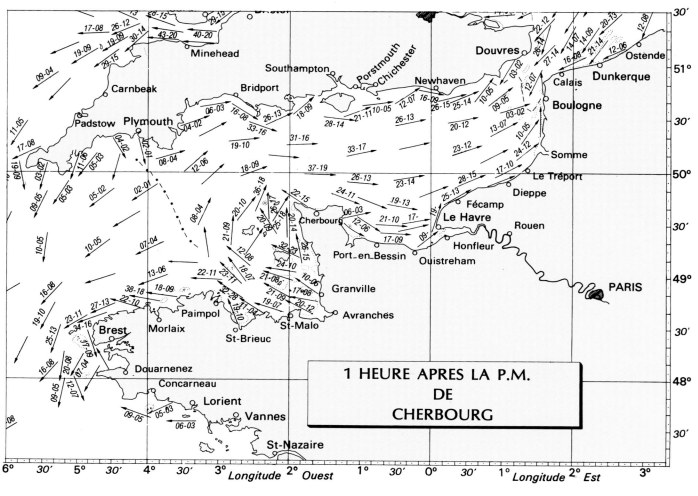

1 HEURE APRES LA P.M.
DE
CHERBOURG

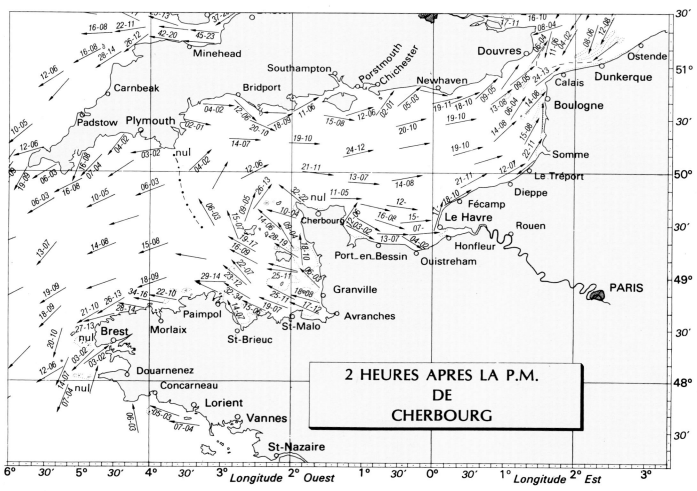

2 HEURES APRES LA P.M.
DE
CHERBOURG

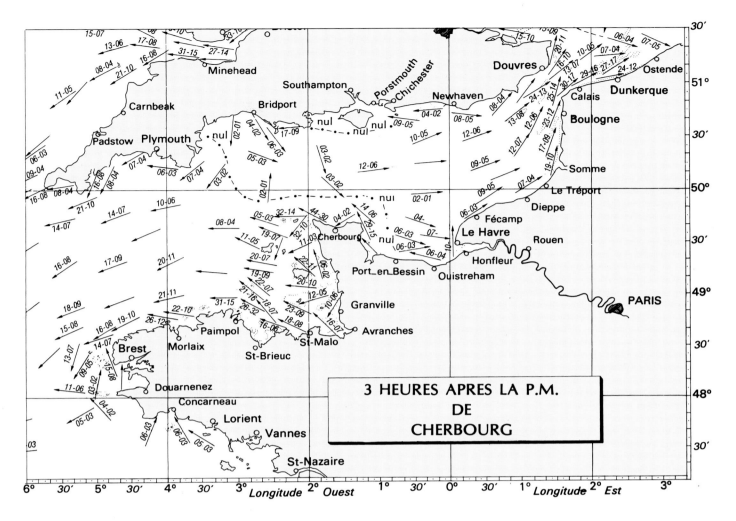

3 HEURES APRES LA P.M.
DE
CHERBOURG

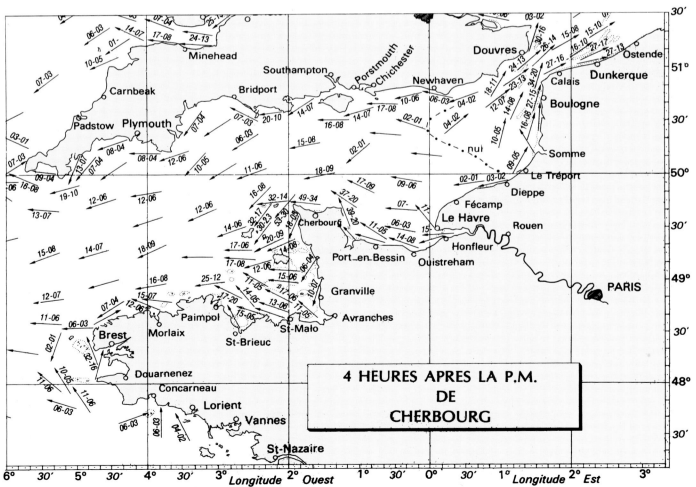

4 HEURES APRES LA P.M.
DE
CHERBOURG

75

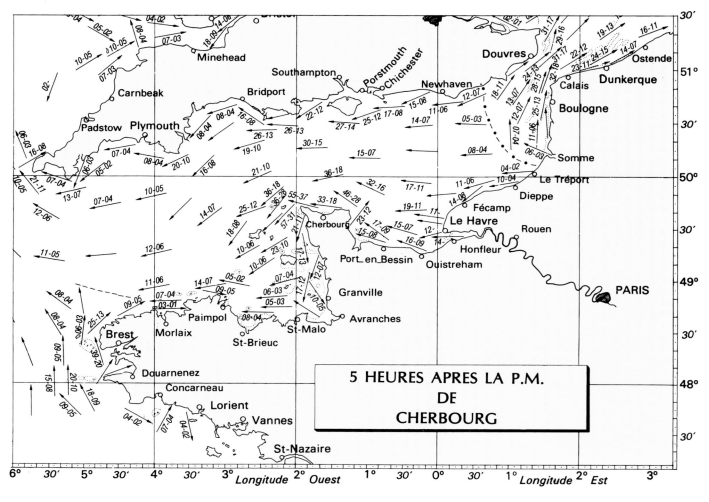

5 HEURES APRES LA P.M.
DE
CHERBOURG

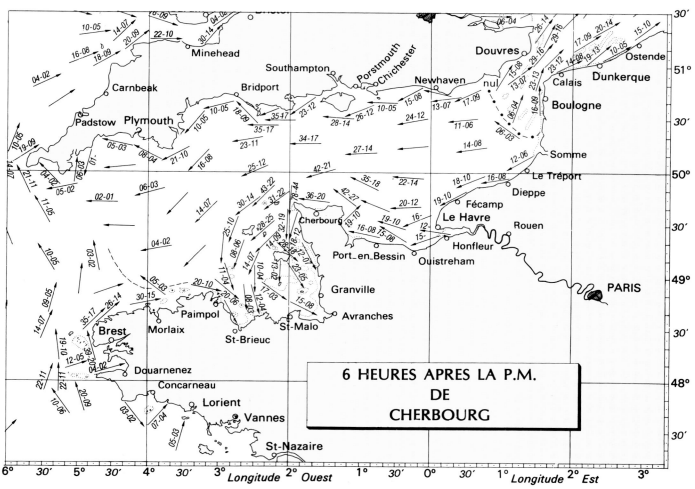

6 HEURES APRES LA P.M.
DE
CHERBOURG

Tidal Streams
Ushant and West Brittany

Based on High Water Brest

The chartlets reproduced here are by the kind permission of SHOM (Le Service Hydrographique et Océanographique de la Marine — Paris) and are taken from Atlas de Courants de Marée No 554.
   The stream rate for springs and neaps is shown adjacent to the directional arrows. A more precise rate can be obtained by the use of the tidal-coefficient system which is published by SHOM and available from BP 426 - 29275 Brest Cedex France.

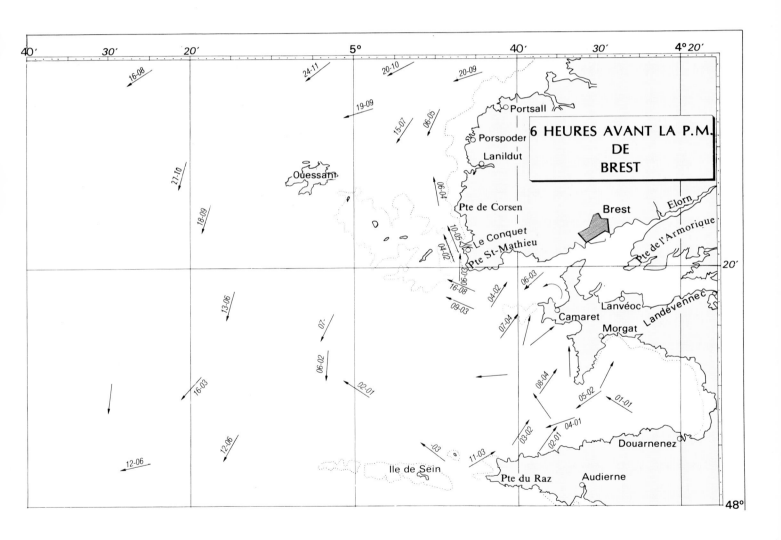

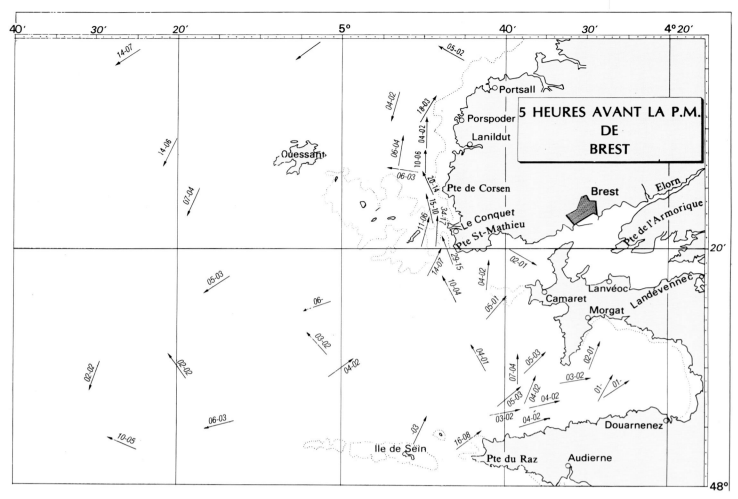

5 HEURES AVANT LA P.M.
DE
BREST

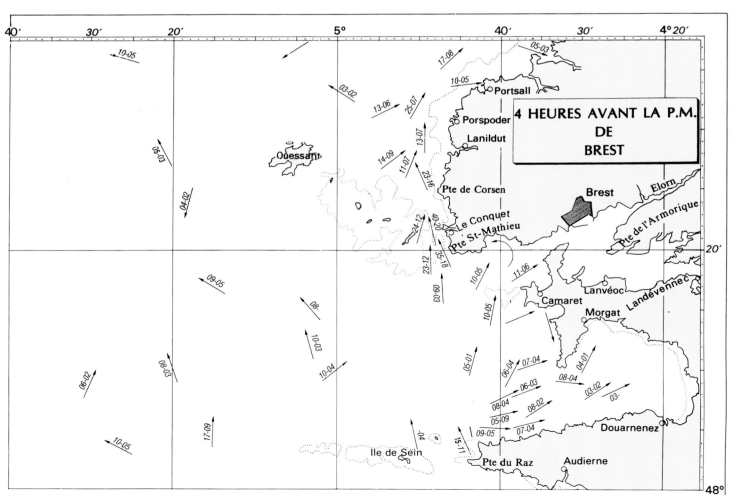

4 HEURES AVANT LA P.M.
DE
BREST

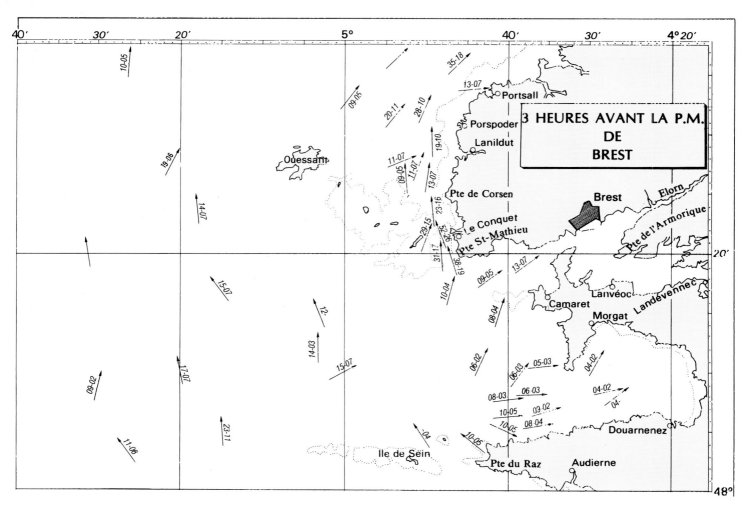

3 HEURES AVANT LA P.M. DE BREST

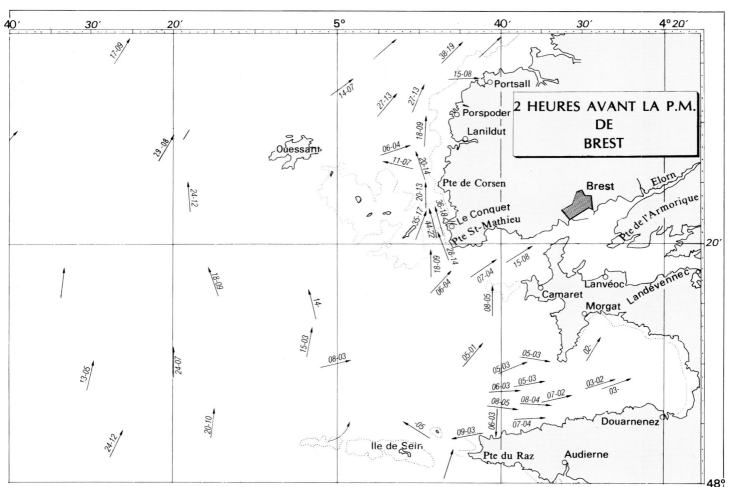

2 HEURES AVANT LA P.M. DE BREST

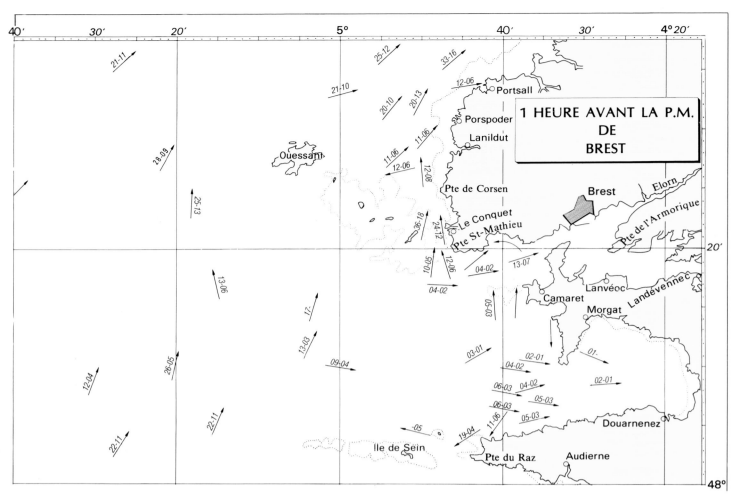

1 HEURE AVANT LA P.M.
DE
BREST

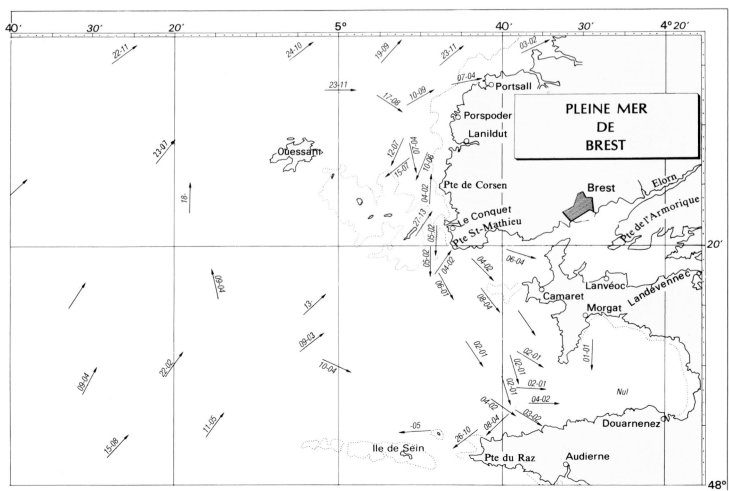

PLEINE MER
DE
BREST

80

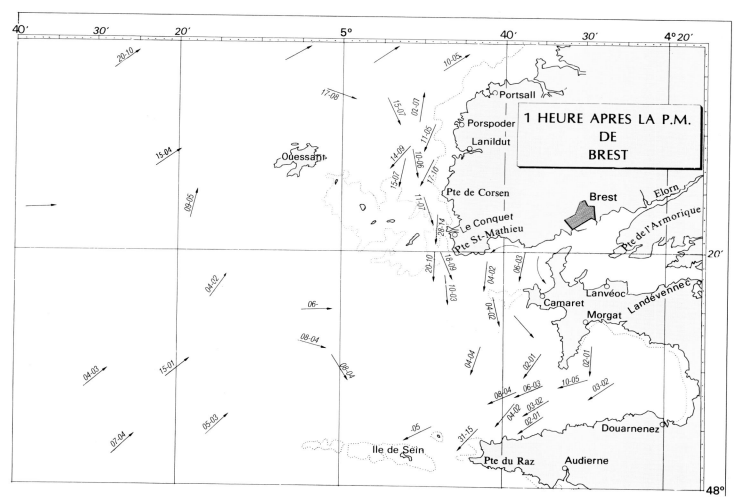

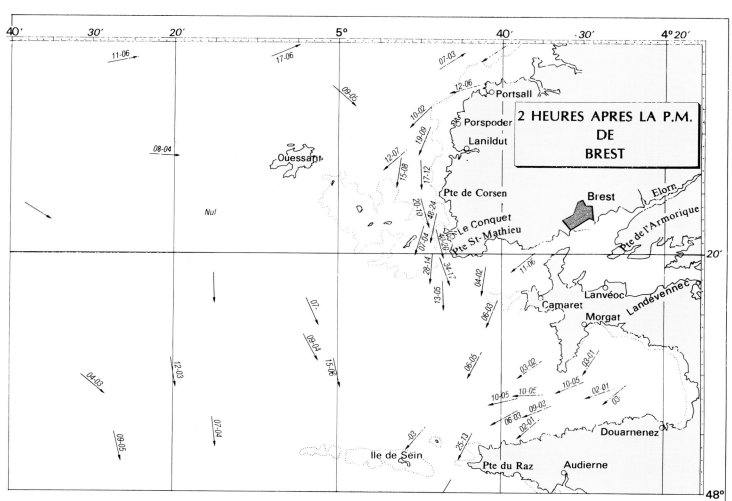

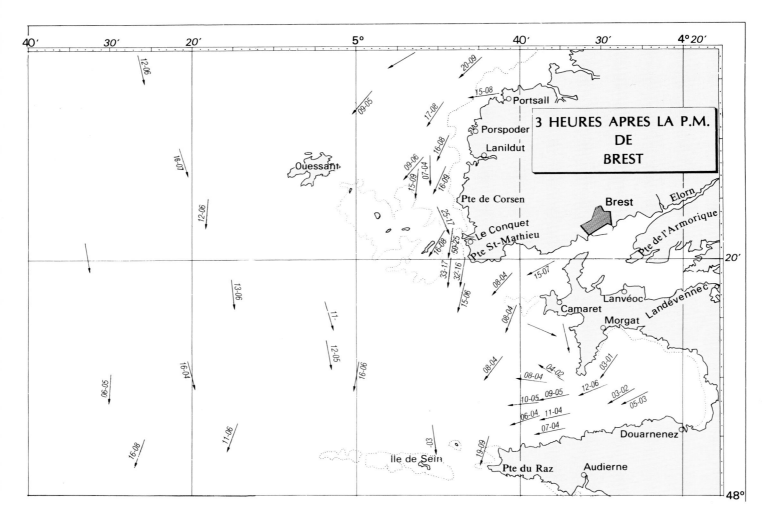

3 HEURES APRES LA P.M.
DE
BREST

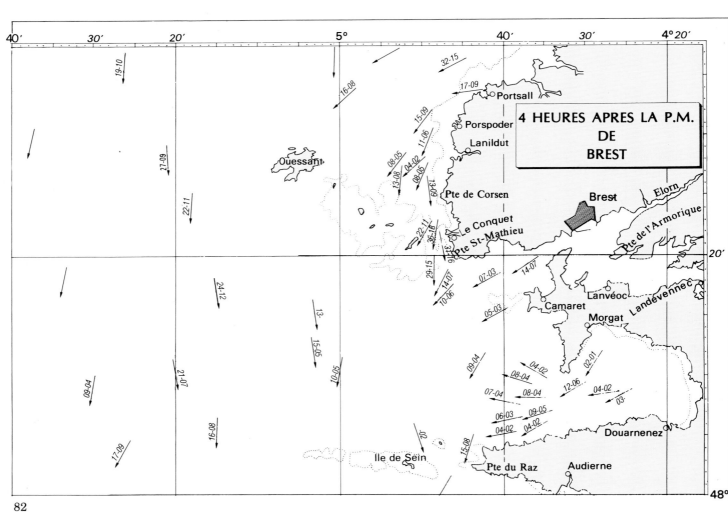

4 HEURES APRES LA P.M.
DE
BREST

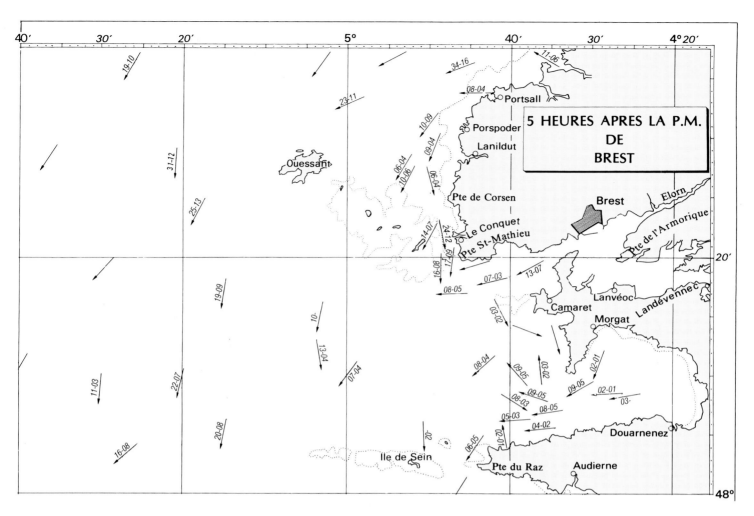

5 HEURES APRES LA P.M. DE BREST

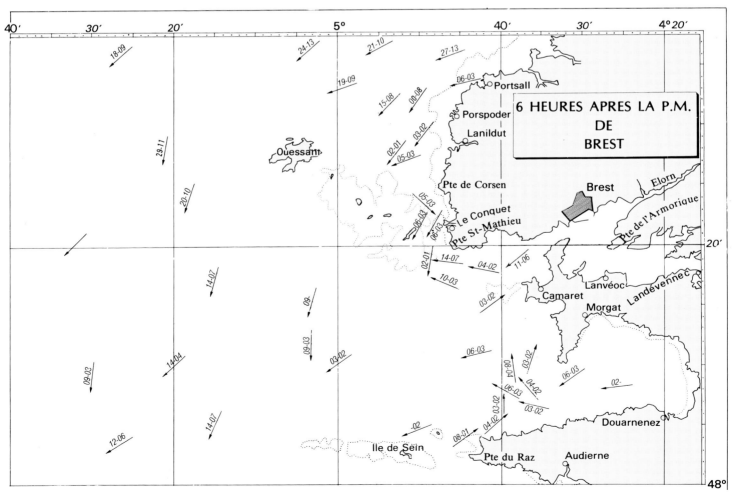

6 HEURES APRES LA P.M. DE BREST

Tidal Streams
Rade de Brest

Based on High Water Brest

The chartlets reproduced here are by the kind permission of SHOM (Le Service Hydrographique et Océanographique de la Marine — Paris) and are taken from Atlas de Courants de Marée No 555.

The stream rate for springs and neaps is shown adjacent to the directional arrows. A more precise rate can be obtained by the use of the tidal-coefficient system which is published by SHOM and available from BP 426 - 29275 Brest Cedex France.

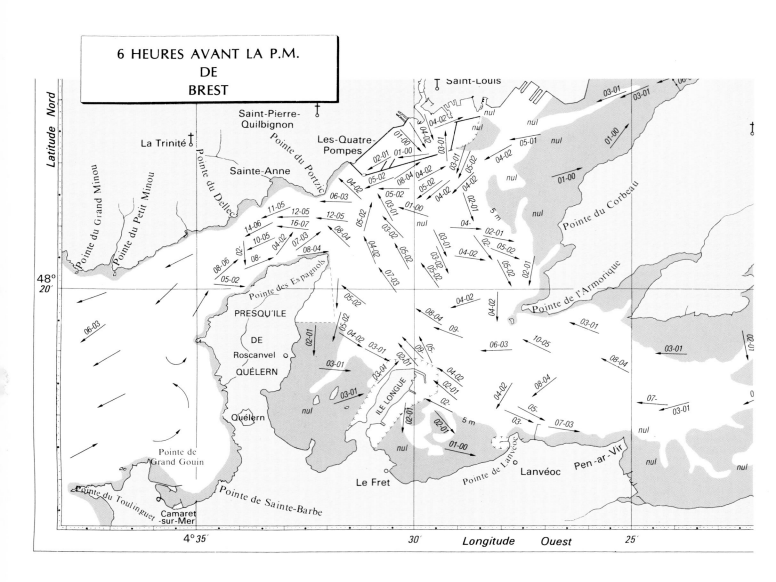

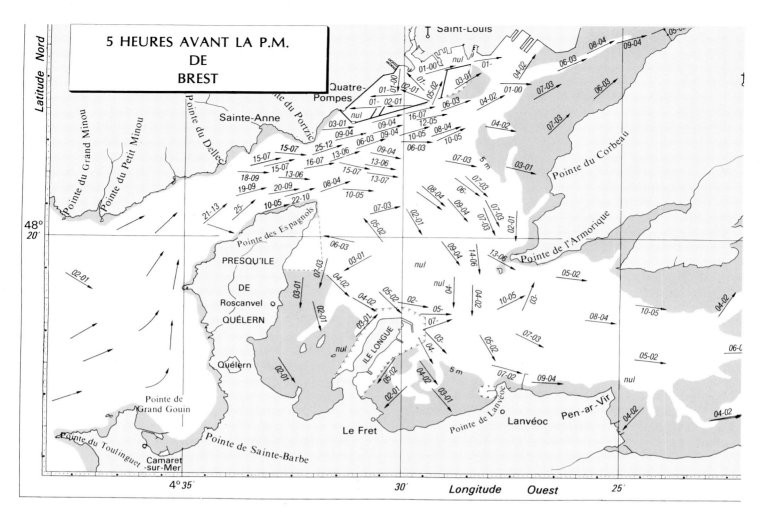

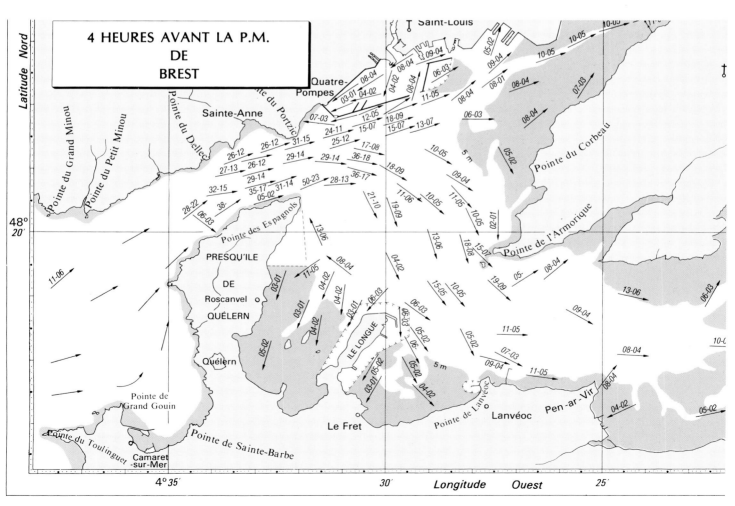

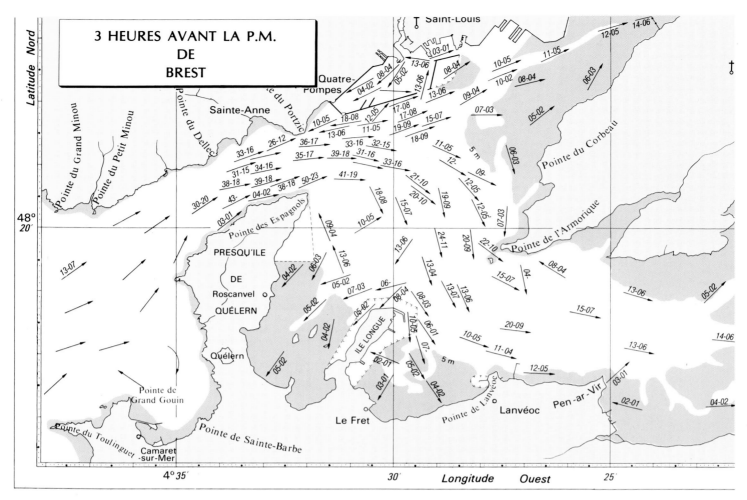

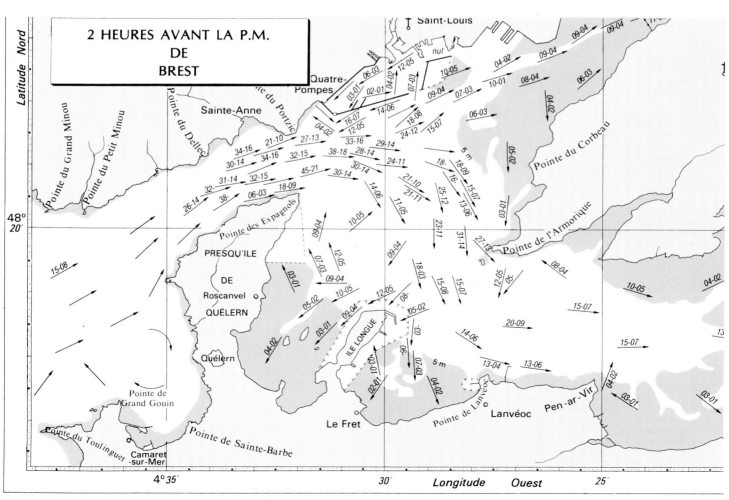

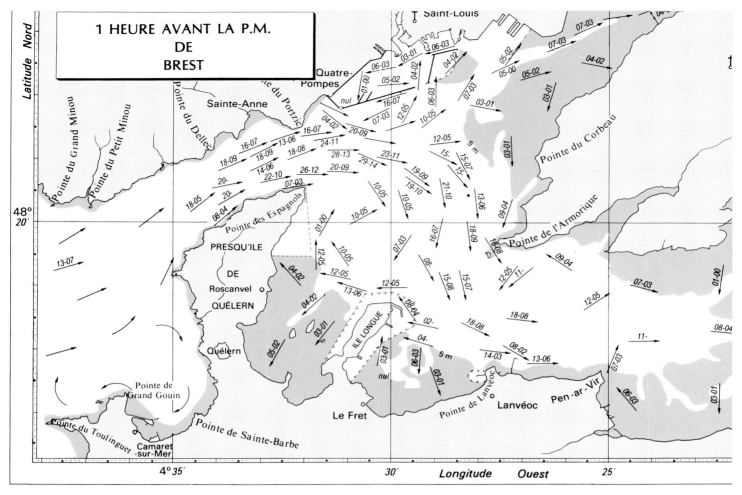

1 HEURE AVANT LA P.M. DE BREST

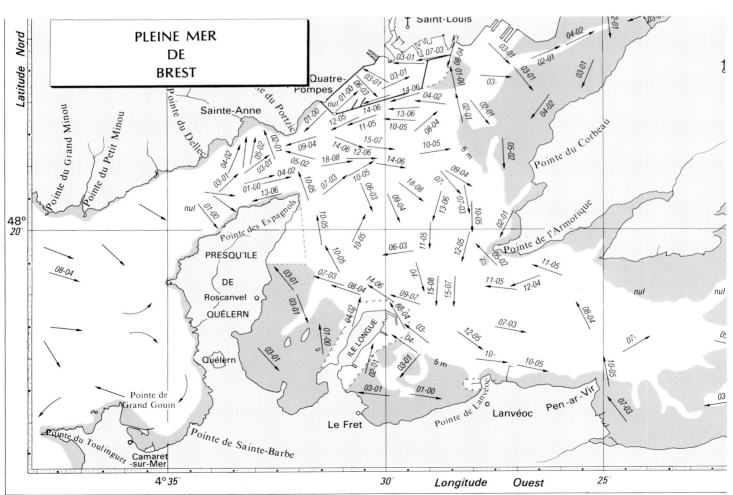

PLEINE MER DE BREST

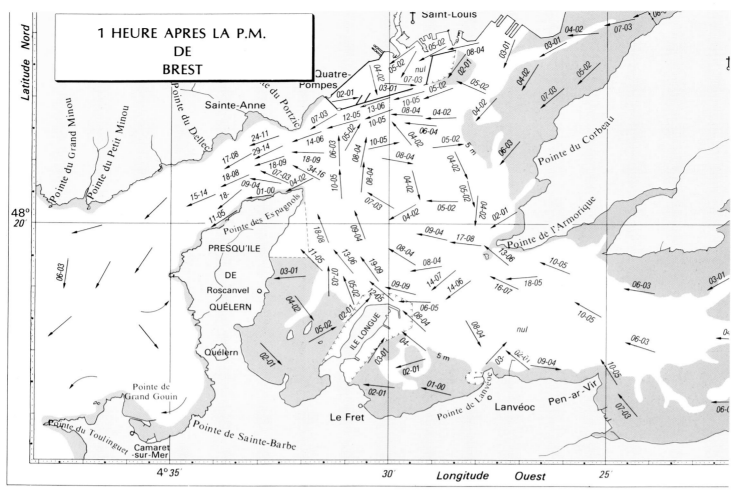

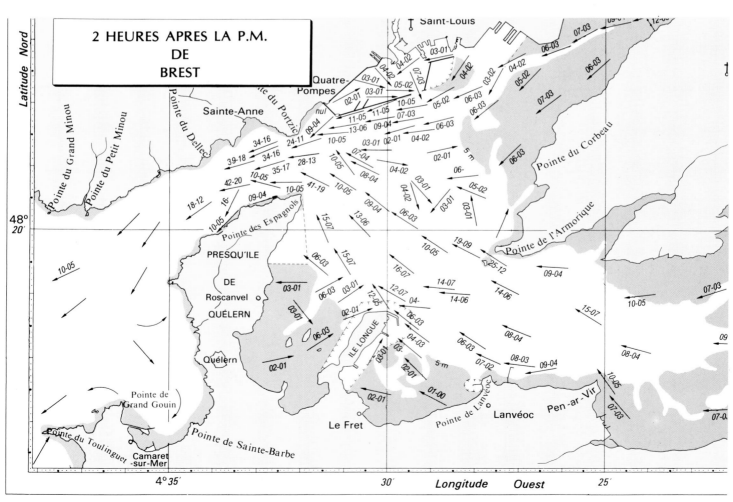

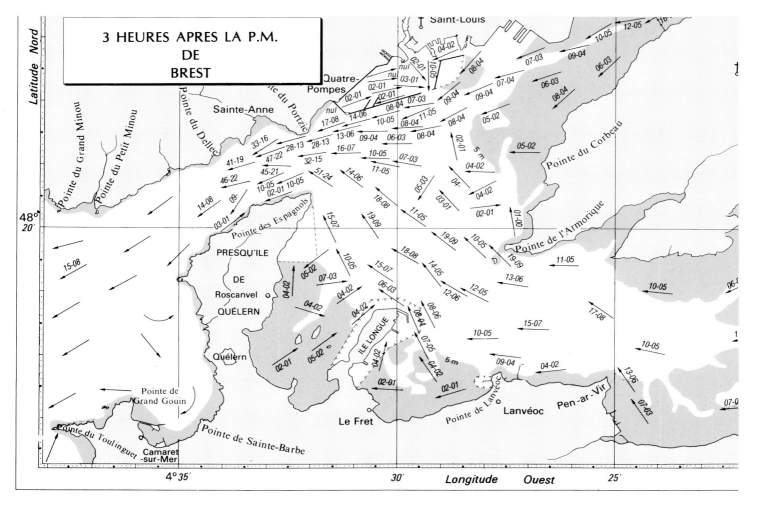

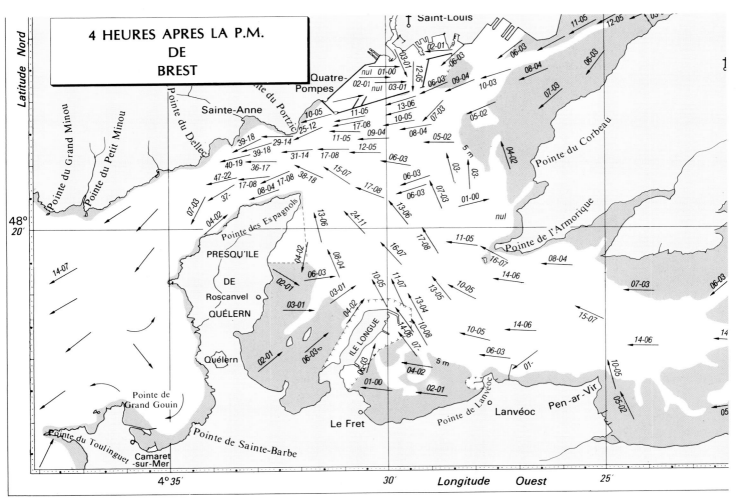

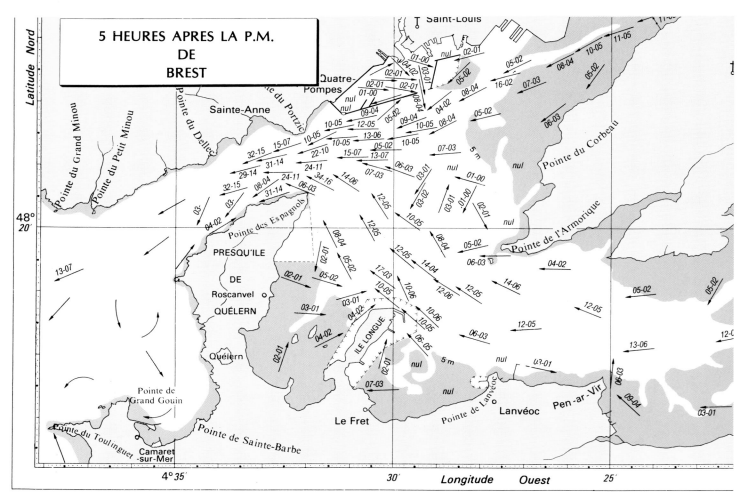

5 HEURES APRES LA P.M.
DE
BREST

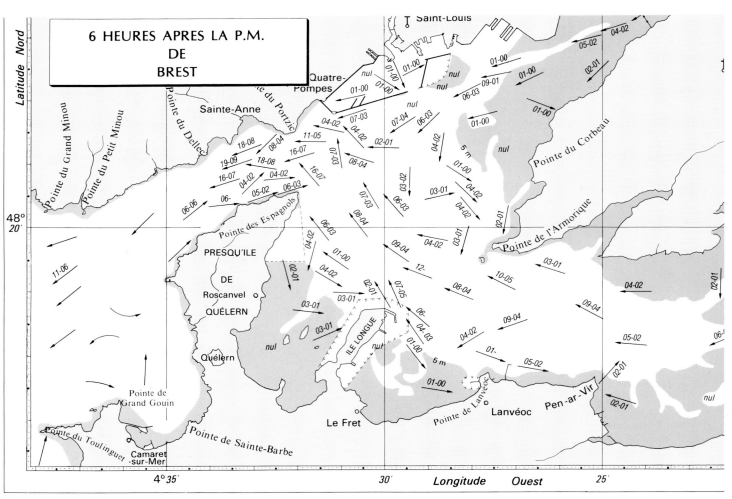

6 HEURES APRES LA P.M.
DE
BREST

Tidal Streams
Southern Brittany

Based on High Water Brest

The chartlets reproduced here are by the kind permission of SHOM (Le Service Hydrographique et Océanographique de la Marine — Paris) and are taken from Atlas de Courants de Marée No 552.

The stream rate for springs and neaps is shown adjacent to the directional arrows. A more precise rate can be obtained by the use of the tidal-coefficient system which is published by SHOM and available from BP 426 - 29275 Brest Cedex France.

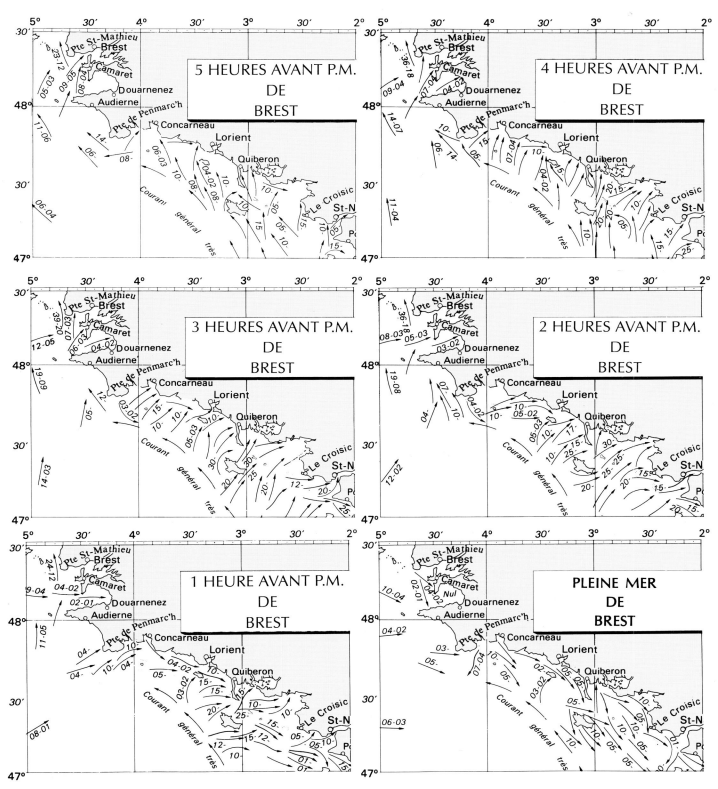

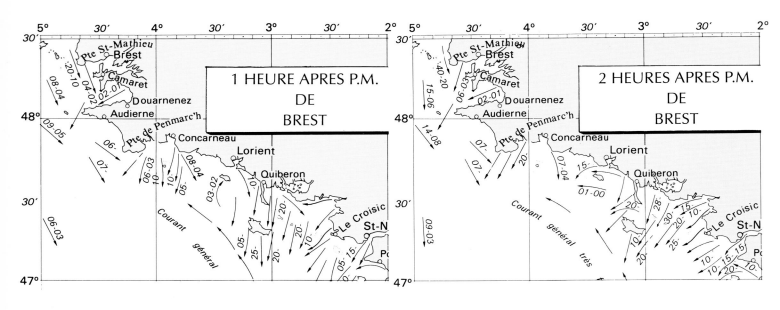

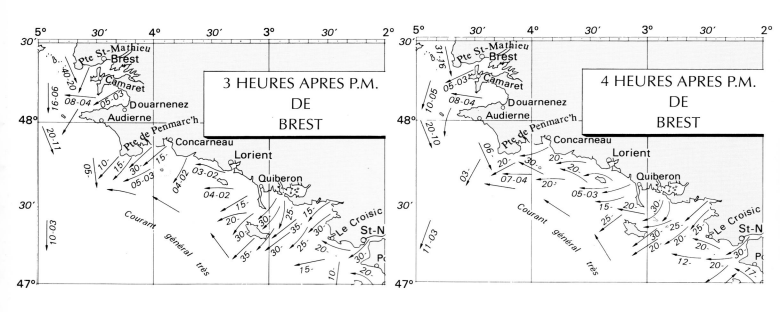

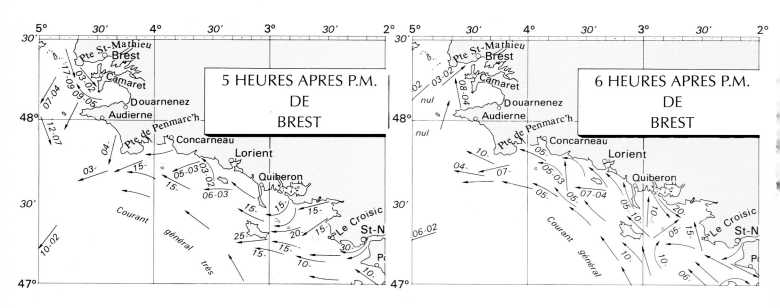

English — French Glossary

ANCHORING, MOORING and PILOTAGE

anchor	l'ancre
anchorage	le mouillage
bank	le banc
bay	l'anse, la baie
beacon	la balise, l'amer
bollard	la bitte
buoy	la bouée
channel	le chenal, la passe
current	le courant
depth	la profondeur
deviation	la déviation
draught	le tirant d'eau
dredged channel	chenal dragué
drying-legs	les béquilles
ebb tide	marée descendante
entrance	l'entrée
estuary	l'estuaire
flood tide	marée montante
high water	la pleine mer
knot	le noeud
ladder	l'échelle
landing slip	la cale
landmark or beacon	l'amer
leading line	l'alignement
least depth	la profondeur minimum
light	le feu
lighthouse	le phare
lock	l'écluse
lock keeper	l'éclusier
low water	la basse mer
mooring buoy	le corps-mort
mooring prohibited	l'accostage interdite
mussel beds	le parc à moules
navigation lights	les feux de navigation
neaps	les mortes eaux
overfalls	les remous et clapotis
oyster beds	le parc à huitres
radio beacon	le radio phare
range (of tide)	l'amplitude
rocks	les rochers
sea level	le niveau
shoal	le haut fond
slack water	la marée étale
spring tide	la vive-eau
tidal race	le raz, les remous violents
tower, beacon tower	la tour
transit	l'alignement
variation	la déclinaison
warp	l'amarre
withies	les osiers
wreck	l'épave

TYPE OF SEA BED

clay (Cy)	l'argile (Arg.)
gravel (G)	le gravier (Gr.)
hard (h)	dur (d)
mud (M)	la vase (V.)
pebbles (P)	cailloux (Caill.)
rock (R)	la roche (R.)
sand (S)	le sable (S.)
shingle (Sn)	les galets (Gal.)
soft (so)	mou (m)
stones (St)	les pierres (Pi.)

WEATHER

anticyclone	l'anticyclone
breeze	la brise
calm	la calme
deepen	se creuser
depression	la dépression
dry	sec
fine	beau temps
fog	le brouillard
front - cold, warm	le front - froid, chaud
gale	le coup de vent
haze	la brume de beau temps
mist	la brume légère
rain	la pluie
ridge	la dorsale
rough sea	mer agitée
storm	la tempête
thunderstorm	l'orage
visibility	la visibilité
— good	bonne
— moderate	modéré
— poor	mauvaise
waves	les vagues
wet	humide

Brittany coast weather forecasts

Telephone forecasts
You can telephone 36 65 08 08 from anywhere around the French coast for Météo France recorded forecasts.

Local coast radio stations
Jersey Radio:
Forecasts for the Channel Islands area, which includes the French coast from Cap de la Hague round to Les Heaux.
VHF channels 25 and 82 at 0645, 0745, 1245, 1845 and 2245 GMT.

St Malo Radio:
Local forecasts on VHF channel 2 at 0633 and 1433 GMT.

Paimpol Radio:
Local forecasts on VHF channel 84 at 0633 and 1433 GMT.

Plougasnou Radio:
Local forecasts on VHF channel 83 at 0633 and 1433 GMT.

Ushant Radio:
Local forecasts on VHF channel 82 at 0633 and 1433 GMT.

Brest Le Conquet:
Local forecasts on VHF channel 26 at 0633 and 1433 GMT.

Pont l'Abbé Radio:
Local forecasts on VHF channel 27 at 0633 and 1433 GMT.

Belle Ile Radio:
Local forecasts on VHF channel 87 at 0633 and 1433 GMT.

St Nazaire Radio:
Area forecasts from the Seine estuary to the Vendée coast. VHF channel 23 at 0633 and 1433 GMT.

Index